EVERY RELATIONSHIP HAS CONFLICT. THE KEY IS TO HANDLE IT CONSTRUCTIVELY.

• Tom wants to spend the family's vacation with his parents at their Florida condo. His wife Susan wants them to go to Mexico. Their positions are miles apart. Can they both get what they want? Find out how in Chapters 6 and 7.

• Tom forgot Susan's birthday. She's ready to explode. What's the other option that can stop this fight before it starts—and stop Susan's hurt? Find out what to do in Chapter 11.

• Your partner is angry and on the attack. Should you fight back? Or do you want to know the strategies that will defuse the situation—and change the negative dynamics in your relationship forever. See Chapter 12.

• Your partner won't negotiate. Can you change things alone? What are your options—and how effective can you be? Chapter 13 lays it out and helps you be the force that makes the difference.

• Your partner acts like the romance is gone. Can you make an indifferent spouse into a lover again? Wooing and winning are negotiating techniques with big rewards in Chapter 17.

BIG ISSUES ... SMALL CONCERNS
SOLVE THEM WITH CONFLICT MANAGEMENT
AND MAKE BOTH OF YOU WINNERS, NOT LOSERS, IN LOVE.

HOW TO MAKE PEACE WITH YOUR PARTNER

Please turn page
for endorsements from the experts ...

"Immensely engaging and encouraging. Connie Peck has produced a 'user friendly' book which carefully and clearly teaches skills to improve couple relationships, no matter how troubled they are. With this knowledge, we can now choose to manage conflict constructively so that both parties win."

—Margot Prior, professor of clinical psychology,
LaTrobe University and University of Melbourne
and chief psychologist, Royal Children's Hospital

"Readable, practical, and easily grasped . . . readers will feel confident and enthusiastic about embarking on the new learning. By applying good conflict resolution skills in a marital partnership, readers cannot help but learn how to better solve conflicts 'out in the world' too—and that has to be good for all of us!"

—Dr. Ann Sanson, developmental psychologist,
coordinator of psychologists for the prevention of
war, Senior Lecturer, University of Melbourne

"At a time when more couples are giving up on loving and caring relationships, Connie Peck's exciting new book offers a splendid ray of hope! The tone of this fine book is upbeat and helpful. . . . Congratulations are in order!"

—Jeffrey Z. Rubin, professor of psychology
and diplomacy, Tufts University

"A great book! Practical and easy to follow . . . warm and constuctive."
—Gary Hankins, Ph.D, author
of *Prescription for Anger*

✦

CONNIE PECK, PH.D., teaches diplomats negotiating and conflict resolution skills through the United Nations Institute for Training and Research where she coordinates the Fellowship Program in Peacemaking and Preventive Diplomacy. A clinical psychologist, she has also taught conflict management skills to her patients and to fellow psychologists. Her book on negotiating, *I Win, You Win*, was a 1993 Australian bestseller. In Australia, she was coordinator of the psychology clinic at La Trobe University, Melbourne, for fifteen years, founding chairperson of the La Trobe University Institute for Peace Research, and the founder and national convenor of Psychologists for the Prevention of War, a special interest group of the Australian Psychological Society. An American citizen, Connie Peck is currently residing in France as part of her international work in teaching negotiating skills.

✦

HOW TO MAKE PEACE WITH YOUR PARTNER

A Couple's Guide to Conflict Management

CONNIE PECK, PH.D.

WARNER BOOKS

A Time Warner Company

WARNER BOOKS EDITION

Cover design by Diane Luger

Warner Books, Inc.
1271 Avenue of the Americas
New York, NY 10020

 A Time Warner Company

Printed in the United States of America

First Printing: June, 1995

10 9 8 7 6 5 4 3 2 1

HOW TO MAKE PEACE WITH YOUR PARTNER

Contents

I. Understanding the Peace Process		*1*
1. Learning to Live with Somebody Who Isn't You		*3*
2. Understanding How Conflicts Escalate		*8*
3. Running Away from Conflict		*17*
4. Negotiating Relationship Rules Based on		
Principles of Fairness		*23*
5. Discovering Wise Ways to Win		*30*
II. Basic Negotiating		*37*
6. Turning Arguments into Negotiations		*39*
7. Understanding Your Partner's Needs		
and Concerns		*44*
8. Being Assertive About Your Needs and Concerns		*56*
9. Finding Common Ground and Brainstorming		
Creative Options		*63*
10. Building Win-Win Solutions		*71*
11. Managing Your Own Emotions		*81*

12. Handling Your Partner's Emotions   95
13. Generalizing Your Negotiation Skills   101

III. Building a Lasting Peace   121

14. Reexamining Your Thinking About Your
Partner and Relationship   123
15. Turning Complaints About the Past into
Requests for the Future   136
16. Putting an End to Dirty Tricks   153
17. Making Love, Not War   171

IV. Yes, But . . .   187

18. Keeping Outside Pressures Outside Your
Relationship   189
19. Tackling the "Hot" Issues and the Serious
Relationship Problems   200
20. Renegotiating Relationship Roles   221
21. Seeking Help from a Third Party   232
22. Meeting the Challenge of Making It Work   239
Skills Review   243
Further Reading   256
References   261

I

Understanding
the
Peace
Process

1

Learning to Live with Somebody Who Isn't You

Learning to live with another person is probably one of the hardest things on earth to do. No matter how similar two people are, they will have some differences in needs, preferences, habits, and beliefs. And such differences inevitably lead to conflict. Ironically, the more intimate the relationship, the more potential there is for conflict.

Some couples believe that if they argue frequently, it is an indication that they no longer love each other. But in fact the opposite is usually true. People argue because they *do* care and because they want to solve their problems. They also argue because they don't know how to resolve their problems any other way. Other couples avoid conflict because they fear it. But by suppressing their differences, they eventually begin to feel isolated and distant from each other, as their needs remain undiscussed and unmet.

This book is for couples who argue too much and for those who don't argue enough. In both cases, partners are likely to end up feeling hurt, angry, and frustrated, because they don't feel listened to and because their needs are not being met. Often, they feel deprived of the most important need of all—the need to be loved.

Contrary to popular belief, conflict is not always a bad thing. It is a normal and unavoidable part of all human interaction. If handled constructively, it is even beneficial, since it can lead to the adjustments necessary to keep a relationship healthy and responsive to the needs of both partners.

However, conflict does cause problems when handled destructively, by being: 1) allowed to escalate out of control or 2) suppressed.

The real problem, therefore, is not how frequently conflict occurs, but how it is managed. Learning to manage conflict does not mean getting rid of it—which, even if it were possible, would be undesirable. Instead, it means learning to handle it constructively rather than destructively.

Conflict Can Be Understood

For a long time, conflict and its causes were poorly understood. But over the past twenty years, social scientists have studied it and discovered ways in which it can be resolved. They have learned that conflict *can* be understood and that certain skills can dramatically facilitate its resolution. Moreover, they have found that these same skills can be learned by most people and applied to most disputes.

Conflict-resolution skills are now used in a wide range of settings. Books and courses on negotiation for businesspeople abound. Mediation and conciliation are being applied to divorce settlements, neighborhood arguments, industrial disputes, disagreements between vested-interest groups, and even international tensions. Some authors have suggested that we are at the beginning of a quiet revolution in how conflict is managed in our society. But news of this revolution has not yet reached many people where they need it most—in their relationships with their partners.

This book draws on the latest conflict-management research, theory, and practice to teach couples how to negotiate satisfactory solutions to their relationship problems. Couples who follow these recommendations will need to learn new skills and to unlearn some old habits. As with any new skill, conflict management requires practice and the kind of feedback that comes from careful evaluation of what one has done well and what one could have done better.

The skills discussed in the following chapters will be most effective if *both* partners read the book carefully and agree to try the techniques. Change in a relationship is always easier and faster when both parties use the same rules and work together. One particularly effective way to do this is to read the book together—aloud. However, in doing so, you will have to be careful not to use this as an opportunity to point out each other's faults.

Sometimes, one partner may be unable or unwilling even to consider change. One common reason is fear or concern about what change in the relationship may bring. If this is the case in your relationship, you can apply the conflict-management skills on your own. If your spouse won't read this book, you can explain the steps so that he or she will understand the process and can participate in it with you.

Accepting Responsibility for Making Your Relationship Better

The philosophy espoused in this book is that each partner should take responsibility for improving the relationship by changing his or her *own* behavior. When partners are in conflict, they usually feel that most of their problems are the other person's fault. Thus, much of their time and effort is spent on trying to persuade or coerce the other person to change. But lasting change can never be forced onto another person. Try as they might, partners who use coercive tactics in an attempt to influence each other's behavior usually end up feeling extremely frustrated.

Richard Stuart, in his book *Helping Couples Change,* has suggested an ingenious way for partners to bring about change in each other. His idea—based on the fact that people always have more control over their own behavior than over another person's, and based on the interactive nature of relationships—is that since relationships are interactive, change in one partner will automatically cause change in the other. Therefore, the best way for you to create change in your spouse is for you to change first. A positive change usually brings about a positive response; a negative change, a negative response. This process is easy to see in your own behavior. If you give me a hug, I'm more likely to want to hug you back. If you shout at me, I'm more likely to shout back at you. This also applies in reverse: If I give you a hug, you're more likely to want to hug me back; if I remain calm, you're more likely to remain calm.

Thus, if you want change in your partner's behavior, the surest way to bring it about is by changing your own behavior. If you want your partner to meet more of your needs, the best strategy is to try to meet more of his or her needs, so that your partner will *want* to reciprocate.

Accepting responsibility for changing your behavior does not mean that you must agree to meet all of your spouse's needs or that you will have to meet needs that are in conflict with your own. Accepting responsibility for change means that when your needs are in conflict, you will try to initiate and follow the negotiation methods presented in this book. It also means learning to express your needs clearly so that your partner will be able to understand them.

Taking responsibility for changing your behavior can be an exciting challenge, and you will gain a sense of pride in acting rationally and maturely. But it may take a little time to break down the wall of suspicion and anger that has built up between you and your partner. Nonetheless, if you are persistent, your spouse will see that you are genuinely trying to make the relationship better, and this will have a positive effect on your relationship.

In conclusion, most conflicts in intimate relationships stem from the unmet needs of one or both partners. Many people have never learned how to ask for their needs to be met or to understand and meet the needs of their partner. Because of the interactive nature of relationships, getting one's needs met and meeting one's partner's needs are often interrelated.

The negotiation method presented here will offer ways to do both. It will not, however, provide instant answers or work like a magic wand. It will require hard work and a commitment to change. Couples who take the time to understand these skills and who conscientiously try to put them into practice will find that their skills become better over time—and so will their relationships.

Before discussing how to go about resolving relationship conflict, it is important to understand how conflict can become destructive.

2

Understanding How
Conflicts Escalate

Often conflict escalates out of control in a seemingly unpredictable and arbitrary way, but in fact it functions according to certain recognizable patterns. Becoming familiar with these patterns is the first step.

The Problem with Arguing Over Positions

Conflicts can range from disagreements over issues of real substance to unimportant differences in style. As will be discussed later, people occasionally have conflicts over the wrong issue or with the wrong person. But the most common type of conflict occurs when partners disagree or want something different. For example:

- Susan wants to go to Mexico for their vacation; Tom wants to go to his parents' condominium in Florida.

- Tom wants another child; Susan doesn't.
- Susan wants Tom to "take more responsibility" around the house; Tom feels that he already does more than his share.
- Susan wants the radio on; Tom doesn't feel like listening to music.
- Tom believes that the kids should be given "a good whack" when they are disobedient; Susan thinks that they should be "reasoned with."
- Susan wants to spend Thanksgiving with her parents; Tom wants to spend it with his family.
- Tom hates having dirty dishes lying around; Susan can't understand why it's such a big deal.

These are examples of "conflicts of interest," as both partners' needs or interests are in conflict. But couples often ignore these differences and try instead to resolve them by arguing over positions. "Positional arguing" occurs when each party adopts a position to represent his or her interests and tries to convince the other that this position is superior. Both partners present reasons to support their conclusion while at the same time arguing against the other's. Susan and Tom, for example, had a long-standing argument about moving. Susan wanted to move to a bigger house. Tom wanted to stay in their current house. Like many couples, they spent hours arguing for and against moving, with little progress and considerable frustration and upset on both sides.

In spite of the hours spent in heated debate, the real needs, wants, and concerns behind each person's position remained unexplored. For example, Susan wanted to move so that she could have her own study, more room to entertain, and a more modern house to project the right kind of image. Tom was concerned about the expense of a new house, liked being close to his work, and (having moved often as a child) wanted the security of remaining in one place. Until these underlying interests are taken into account, Tom and Susan are unlikely to find a satisfactory solution to their problem.

In positional arguing, these underlying needs and concerns are seldom explored in a systematic fashion. When they are mentioned in the attempts at mutual persuasion, they are viewed as arguments aimed at winning, and because of the context in which they are presented, they are not fully appreciated as genuine needs or concerns.

A second problem with this kind of arguing is that each position is only one of many possible ways to meet each person's needs. Because each party becomes so focused on advocating his or her own position and disputing the other's, new or creative ideas about how the problem might be solved are never discussed. Moreover, when people know that they will have to argue for a position, they sometimes choose one that is more extreme than they would have otherwise selected, in order to give themselves some "bargaining" room. Strangely, when people defend a position, they often become even more committed to it than they had intended. The more they argue, the harder they find it to move to a new position— even when it becomes clear that a different one might be in their best interest. Thus, they become "entrapped" by their commitment to defending a particular position.

The result of this is that new ideas that might be acceptable to both parties are never even explored; instead, the couple becomes involved in a battle of wills or power struggle over their positions. If neither side concedes, or even if one side does concede, the conflict may be repeated, since needs remain unfulfilled. Usually, the best solution in positional arguing is a compromise, which is not very satisfactory to either side. Solutions where both sides win occur rarely because neither side has taken the time to examine or understand his or her real needs and concerns or those of the partner. Moreover, neither party will have considered all of the possible options for meeting its own needs, and it is even more unlikely that either will have contemplated trying to satisfy the needs of the other.

No matter how the couple approaches a positional argument or what their positions are, positional arguing is unlikely to lead to satisfactory solutions. Consider this example in which Susan tries to talk to Tom about her desire to do something different for their vacation.

SUSAN: (Tentatively) I've been thinking about our vacation this year and I think we should go somewhere different.

TOM: Like where?

SUSAN: Like Mexico. I've heard it's interesting.

TOM: Mexico? That would cost a bundle! What's wrong with doing what we always do?

SUSAN: (Becoming angry) Because what we always do is boring! If you think I enjoy spending my vacation babysitting your parents, you're wrong!

TOM: You've never complained before. . . .

SUSAN: Oh yes I did! I tried to suggest that we go somewhere else last year, but you said it would be too expensive.

TOM: (Defensively) I don't remember that.

SUSAN: That's because you never listen to me. You just go ahead and do whatever you want. Well, I'm sick of it!

TOM: That's not fair. Besides, I don't always get my way.

SUSAN: You have for the last five years!

TOM: We couldn't afford to do what you wanted. You never consider these things!

SUSAN: At least I'm not a cheapskate like you. All you ever think about is money, money, money! If I had known that when I married you, I would have had second thoughts.

TOM: There are lots of things I know now that would have made *me* think twice.

SUSAN: Oh yeah—like what?

TOM: Like what a nag you are!

SUSAN: You'd make anybody into a nag. What do you think *you* are? You're a tyrant!

As the partners fail to convince each other, they become increasingly frustrated and emotions begin to flare. At this point, the argument may expand to encompass other grievances, with old sources of anger thrown in. Sometimes arguments escalate to involve insults and personal attacks, or they may be sidetracked into a fight about fighting. In any case, the problem is rarely resolved, and even when it is, both partners are likely to end up feeling angry and hurt. Even after they have "made up," resentment can remain. If arguments go this way repeatedly, well-rehearsed patterns soon develop, and the couple becomes like two actors performing the same play over and over. Both say their lines as if on cue, in response to the other's provocation.

Once such patterns are established, even inconsequential issues can escalate out of control. Several factors that contribute to this kind of runaway escalation have been identified.

Each Side Views Its Motivation as "Good" and the Partner's as "Bad"

Because we are much better at understanding our own needs, wants, fears, concerns, motives, and intentions than at understanding those of another person, we see our own behavior as justified and our partner's as unjustified. This causes each partner to assume the worst about the other's intentions and is one of the reasons why conflict escalates so quickly. In the absence of real understanding of the other's motivations, it is easy to believe that one's partner is being critical, hurtful, or purposefully obstructive. The more frequently conflict occurs, the more each partner assumes the worst, and this leads to "conflict spirals."

The Dynamics of Conflict Spirals

Usually, conflict spirals begin when one partner construes the other's behavior as aggressive and, feeling unfairly attacked, counterattacks. But since the other partner does not view his or her behavior as belligerent, the *other's* action is seen as unprovoked and requiring counterattack.

At this point, both sides view the conflict similarly—as the other's "fault." And because each thinks that it was the other side who "started it," each believes that the imbalance can only be rectified when it has the last word. But what each partner views as a justified defense is viewed by the other as yet another round of unprovoked attack, which must be responded to in order to even the score and show that this kind of behavior won't be tolerated. Because the interpretation of the other's behavior is in the eye of the beholder, each partner believes that it is the other one who is escalating the conflict and who wants it to continue. Hence, each believes that the other should be the first to make a move to de-escalate the conflict or to make up. Naturally, neither does so, even though both would like the conflict to end. Conflict spirals are sometimes called "reverberating echoes" or "tit for tat" exchanges, since each party's behavior stimulates a similar response from the other, and the cycle goes on and on. Such spirals often assume a dynamic of their own as the process of attack and counterattack become more important than the issue that started the conflict.

Conflicts Tend to Expand

Even when such arguments begin over substantive issues, they often turn into a "fight about fighting." For example, when a discussion about disciplining the kids turned nasty, Susan accused Tom of shouting at her. Tom replied hotly that he was shouting because *she* was shouting. This led to an argument about who had shouted first. The original conflict over how to discipline the children had changed into a dispute about who was to blame for escalating the argument. Fighting about fighting, which happens commonly, diverts the discussion from a dispute over substance to a dispute over process. It tends to expand the issues and make the argument more immediate and personal, thus increasing the possibilities for personal attacks.

Another factor that tends to exacerbate conflicts is that people tend to attribute their undesirable behavior to circumstances, but to classify their partner's behavior as due to stable (unchangeable) personality traits. Thus, the partner's "inability to make decisions," "dependency," "selfishness," or "lack of maturity" becomes the explanation for his or her behavior. Assigning causes to personality traits in this way tends to make partners less likely to look for and try to understand the circumstances that motivate each other's behavior. Moreover, it causes the person who makes this judgment to feel that there is nothing more to understand. In order to bolster the argument that this is not an isolated instance and to prove that the other *is* selfish or immature, other examples of the perceived personality traits are reviewed. As a result, past grievances are dredged up, and these further expand the argument and confuse the original issue.

Anger Comes from Feeling Unfairly Treated

In attempting to suppress and punish the other's behavior, each party meets the other's attack with an even more vigorous counterattack. The result is that the conflict tends to grow in intensity over time. Emotions become involved as soon as people feel unfairly attacked. Hurt usually comes first, followed by anger about being hurt. But because anger is more apparent than hurt, it is the other's anger that each side sees. Seeing the other person's anger further confirms each side's belief that the other is indeed on the offensive. Such emotions further inflame the conflict.

Intense or Prolonged Conflict Can Permanently Affect the Relationship

When conflict becomes intense, prolonged, or chronic, a change begins to take place in both parties. As anger mounts, each side becomes more aggressive in seeking its goal. Whereas each partner initially wanted only to defend his or her position or self from attack, anger and a growing sense of injustice now cause each to become more intent on punishing or hurting the other. Ironically, each side's original belief that the other was aggressive becomes a reality. At this point, the defensive conflict spiral becomes a retaliatory spiral.

If allowed to go on for long or if taken beyond a certain point, this process can cause an irreversible change in the relationship and in how the partners view it. For example, if, in the heat of battle, Susan told Tom that she has *never* trusted him, or if Tom slapped Susan (which he had never done before), basic attitudes could be permanently changed by these actions. Of course, many couples have battle after battle without this happening, and many couples don't let their conflicts get to this point. But if feuding is continual or if anger goes beyond the couple's normal boundary of "acceptable abuse," the relationship can be seriously damaged.

The essence of runaway conflict escalation is that each side sees the other as the instigator and perpetuator of the conflict. Each believes that the other is on the attack and that his or her own behavior is purely defensive (and therefore justified). Anger, which comes from each side's perception of being unfairly treated, exacerbates the situation, but the hurt and sense of injustice behind the anger go unnoticed. When the conflict intensifies further, punishing the partner can become a more important goal than defending oneself or even winning. If allowed to continue, this malignant process may damage the relationship, perhaps permanently.

It is important to remember that each partner has his or her own interpretation of events, and that it is this interpretation or perception of reality (rather than reality itself) that guides behavior. The major factor that perpetuates conflict is that the parties tend not to understand each other's needs and concerns because they don't listen to each other very carefully. Both are usually so busy trying to convince the other of their own interpretation that they don't hear the other side's perspective. It is sometimes said that parties in a dispute don't communicate enough. But often the problem is not that they don't talk enough—it is that they don't *listen* enough!

When we consider how quickly and intensely conflicts (even about inconsequential matters) can escalate, it sometimes seems unbelievable that conflicts can be handled differently, with very different results. But thankfully, they can be, as will be discussed shortly. First, however, let's look at the dangers of suppressing conflict.

3

Running Away
from Conflict

The belief that conflict is undesirable, and that it doesn't exist in happy marriages, causes some couples to suppress their own and their partner's needs in order to avoid conflict. George Bach and Peter Wyden, in their book *The Intimate Enemy,* classify some partners as "hawks" (those whose tactics escalate arguments as discussed in the last chapter), while they call those who avoid conflict "doves." They are quick to point out, however, that doves (who may think they are keeping the peace) contribute to marital disharmony just as much as hawks do. Moreover, doves do not avoid conflict for noble reasons; they avoid it because they fear it. In fact, some authors refer to this behavior as "fight phobia." Such partners seek appeasement or "peace at any price" and usually concede to the other's wishes or simply ignore them altogether. Unfortunately, avoiding conflict does not make needs disappear or erase differences in needs, and avoidance of conflict will have long-term adverse consequences for relationships in which these tactics are dominant.

Couples Who Don't Fight

Couples who boast that they never fight or argue are not always to be envied. Because they never discuss their needs, wants, and concerns, their relationships do not change to accommodate their differences or changing needs, and therefore their relationships do not grow. Over the long term, partners in this type of relationship are likely to feel frustrated. Since open expression of negative feelings is not "allowed," this frustration gets expressed indirectly—for example, in a passive-aggressive or disguised manner (such as through hinting, negative allusions, or nonverbal expression). In addition, because the source of frustration and even the emotions are suppressed, it is virtually impossible for the partners to understand each other's complaints and to seek satisfactory solutions. Further, when partners suppress needs, they usually experience a decreased sense of intimacy, as the areas that are off-limits for discussion grow. Thus, suppressing conflict tends to limit the relationship and often produces an undercurrent of tension. Not surprisingly, positive feelings also become suppressed as the partners become mutually withdrawn from each other. Over time, they have less and less to talk about. It is their mutual fear of having problems that makes it impossible for them to discuss what is happening or to do anything about it. In fact, it is not uncommon for couples trapped in a pattern of mutual withdrawal to separate without ever acknowledging or discussing there was something wrong!

Complaints and dissatisfactions are inevitable in any relationship and are not in themselves problems. Problems occur when couples don't have the skills to resolve them. The first step in positive handling of dissatisfactions is the ability to discuss them. One author notes that "being able to have problems solves them." Couples who can't discuss problems have been called "deprived," "psychologically malnourished," and "emotionally divorced." Clearly, such behavior does not lead to a satisfying relationship over the long run.

Couples Who Combine Confrontation and Withdrawal

Another common pattern exists when one partner tries to suppress conflict and the other tries to argue. These couples are also unsuccessful in having their needs met, since each person's behavior increases in the other's reciprocal behavior. The avoidant partner's evasion tends to make the confrontational partner more insistent. The confronting partner's direct assault on the issue causes the avoidant partner to want to withdraw even further. These "paired binds" cause the partners to push each other into more and more extreme positions, until their responses become so exaggerated that the couple turn into caricatures of themselves.

Consider the following conversation, in which Susan brings up a topic she wants to discuss, but Tom, fearing conflict, subverts and avoids the discussion:

SUSAN: I've been thinking about our vacation this year and I want to go somewhere different.

TOM: Mmm.

SUSAN: What do you think?

TOM: Let's talk about it later. I have to mow the lawn.

SUSAN: I've heard that Mexico is interesting.

TOM: (Doesn't respond)

SUSAN: What would you think of going to Mexico?

TOM: (Noncommittal and distracted) We'll see.

SUSAN: (Becoming frustrated) I can't stand another holiday with your parents!

TOM: (Gets up and leaves the room)

SUSAN: (Yelling) How come you always leave when I want to talk to you?

TOM: (Returns to the room and says in a patronizing voice) I told you, I have to mow the lawn. It might rain.

SUSAN: When *can* we talk about it then?

TOM: Later.

SUSAN: (Shouting) When? I want to know when!

TOM: Just calm down . . . Why do you get upset so easily? The neighbors will hear you.

SUSAN: I don't care about the neighbors! I want you to promise that we'll talk about it later!

TOM: Sure . . . (Walks out of the house and mows the lawn)

Of course, problems don't get resolved this way either. Susan is left fuming. Not only have her needs about their vacation been dismissed, but even her desire to discuss them has been ignored. There's a good chance that she will bring up the topic again—and that the discussion will be even more emotionally charged and acrimonious. Not only did Tom's desire to smooth everything over fail, but now the conflict that he fears appears inevitable—through his attempts at avoidance.

Couples Who Alternate Confrontation and Avoidance

Another common pattern among couples is to alternate between intense conflict and complete conflict avoidance. A particularly nasty argument usually leads to a period of withdrawal, when the couple assiduously avoids any discussion of the issue for fear of another argument. This approach is equally unsuccessful at satisfying needs, and the avoidance is often followed by yet another (usually abortive) round of complaints, blame, and demands for change.

It is no wonder that spouses become so frustrated with each other that they want to give up. Of course, many people do try to solve their problems by ending the relationship. However, when partners separate, it is almost always because they did not adequately learn how to meet each other's needs. Unfortunately, they often wanted to, but they simply didn't know how.

Living Happily Ever After Means Learning New Skills

Through fairy tales and romantic novels and movies, society sets up the false expectation that once married, we will automatically "live happily ever after." We are told that "marriages are made in heaven" and led to believe that if we can find the right partner, the details will all magically work themselves out—with, of course, the help of true love.

Thus, when things don't magically sort themselves out, we may start to wonder whether our spouse is the "right" person after all, and we may begin to look for someone else who will meet our needs. One of the ways that people deal with this frustration is by imagining ideal situations. But sadly, those who enter a new relationship with the same unrealistic expectations often end up with a whole new set of frustrations and unmet needs.

What we should have been taught is that "living happily ever after" is hard work and requires us to learn new relationship skills. These include knowing how to express our own needs and concerns in a way that is not threatening to our partner, how to listen and respond to our partner's needs and concerns, and how to negotiate conflicts and find solutions that will meet both parties' needs.

The only training in these skills that most people receive comes from observing their parents. For the most part, we learn how to be "hawks" or "doves" from our mothers and fathers. Unfortunately, parents are not always the best role models, and unproductive, coercive, or avoidant methods for managing conflict are often passed on from generation to generation. To complicate the situation further, partners often come to the relationship having learned not only unproductive but often quite different and incompatible ways of approaching conflict. These different styles can themselves become the source of additional stress as new arguments erupt over differences in how conflicts are approached.

Luckily, it is never too late to learn new skills. Unlike old dogs, couples *can* learn new tricks. Listening, assertion, and negotiation skills, which are regularly taught to business executives, should be regularly taught to couples for use at home, since the battles fought in the living room are every bit as important as those waged in the boardroom.

Learning new skills to replace old habits is not easy. New skills must be practiced at the hardest possible times. Sometimes partners may forget to use them or may even choose not to use them. But those who succeed in applying them will find that they become easier with practice. Moreover, couples will find that their increasing satisfaction with their relationship is well worth the effort.

4

Negotiating Relationship Rules Based on Principles of Fairness

In every relationship there are certain privileges (such as receiving affection when one feels the need) and responsibilities (doing the dishes or taking the children to music lessons). Many of these privileges and responsibilities are defined by relationship rules, which each couple develops in its own way. Some rules are explicit and have been discussed openly (for example, who does the dishes), but others are unspoken, having evolved without discussion (for example, who gives affection to whom and when). In many instances, partners are only vaguely aware that these rules exist.

But the exchange of privileges and responsibilities and the rules that govern them are among the most common sources of relationship conflict. Both parties naturally want to maximize the positive benefits and minimize the disadvantages. In fact, these rules of "distributive justice" are so important that much of the research into marital satisfaction is based on what is called "exchange theory."

The most common relationship rules—and also the most common sources of conflict—include those about who does which household chores, who disciplines the children, who makes major life decisions, how money is managed, how time is divided between work and leisure, how affection and sex are handled, how leisure time is spent, how relationships with parents and in-laws are managed, and, finally, how relationships with others outside the marriage are to be treated.

Since some relationship rules are never discussed, where do they originate? Many can be traced to what we learned from observing our parents' relationships. Other sources of learning include our observations of other couples and culturally instilled ideas of how relationships are "supposed" to work. Definitions of sex roles that have been taught to us by our culture (not only by parents, but by school, movies, television, books, magazines, and friends) can have a powerful influence.

But other people's rules are not necessarily right for us. For example, both partners may have learned that it is up to the male to initiate sex, but they may be dissatisfied with this practice. However, because such rules seemed to evolve almost naturally, the underlying assumptions may never have been questioned or discussed.

In cases where the partners have learned different relationship rules, the couple may disagree on what the rules for their relationship should be. For example, one partner may believe that child-rearing responsibilities should be shared equally, while the other believes that they are primarily the woman's responsibility. Differences of this type can lead to conflict in many other areas, without the underlying issue ever being recognized. With so many relationship rules to be worked out, it is no wonder that the first few years of living together are usually difficult.

Problems also occur when one or both parties become dissatisfied with the rules. As partners or circumstances change, old relationship rules may no longer apply. For example, if the female partner takes a full-time job, she may become dissatisfied if there is no change in the former relationship rule that she do most of the housework. Sadly, this discontent is sometimes mistaken for dissatisfaction with the relationship. The result is that partners blame each other instead of addressing the real source of the problem, which is that their relationship rules need to be updated.

Power Balances and Power Struggles

In most relationships, partners maintain a kind of mental balance sheet of privileges and duties. If either party perceives that he or she is getting stuck with too many tasks or that the other is receiving too many privileges or making too many decisions, he or she feels unfairly treated. The fact that each side has its own unique perspective on the situation complicates things further. It is not uncommon for one or even both partners to believe that the other has more power in the relationship and hence to feel a sense of injustice. In fact, many of the struggles in intimate relationships are just that— power struggles.

Power struggles are attempts to readjust the power balance so that each party can feel that he or she is getting a fairer deal. More often than not, these disputes are initiated by the partner who feels at a disadvantage. Frequent power struggles are usually a sign that the relationship rules need some adjustment. It doesn't matter whether differences in power are real or perceived; what is important is how the partners view the situation. Power struggles are like warning signals, and if not heeded and dealt with, they may lead to more severe problems and even to a breakup of the relationship. So, it is important to pay attention to the message behind these power struggles. The decoded message usually translates as: "I think that things are not fair." Behind this may be the even more important message: "I'm worried that you don't care that things are not fair." Often it is difficult to hear this message because it is disguised in an angry, emotional outburst that seems to be an attack on you. It is especially hard to hear it if you are the one who feels treated unfairly. But if you are to get your relationship rules right, so that continual power struggles can be avoided, you will need to hear the real message and to do something about it.

Being in a more powerful position, getting more benefits, and avoiding duties sounds good, but there is always a day of reckoning when the less powerful partner demands to have his or her turn at wielding power, and continuation of the relationship itself may be held to ransom. Sometimes partners quietly leave in search of a more equitable relationship, where the other person *will* care about meeting their needs. Frequently, the partner who has been more powerful is taken completely by surprise, but it may be too late.

Of course, the person who is aggrieved also has a responsibility to put his or her complaints in such a way that the spouse doesn't feel attacked and is able to respond to requests for change. This important skill will be discussed in more detail later.

One reason why partners sometimes feel that the other has greater power is that power imbalances often differ from one issue to another. For example, one person may have more power over the finances, while the other may have more say in deciding whether to have another child. Each is acutely aware of the issues that are a source of his or her dissatisfaction and less aware of the issues that are of concern to the other.

Differences in actual power are not a problem if both parties are happy with their arrangement, and in fact many couples live happily by agreeing to apportion decision-making power to each other in different areas. The important point is that both parties have discussed the arrangement and believe it is fair. So, working out some basic relationship principles can make it easier to work out your relationship rules.

Reciprocity: A Good Guiding Principle

One of the first things to consider is whether you want to adhere to a principle of equality or reciprocity in your relationship. Equality and reciprocity do not mean that you will split everything in half or that you will take turns in making all decisions. Rather these concepts mean that *overall* you will try to achieve a balance of benefits and responsibilities between you. Deciding that you want to accept this principle does not say anything about *how* you will do this—that will be up to you to work out through negotiation. However, what it does suggest is that your relationship rules as a whole should satisfy both of you.

One of the difficulties with establishing reciprocity is that you will be forced to compare apples and oranges—as for example, when you try to decide whether doing the dishes is equal to doing the laundry or whether looking after the lawn is similar to doing the shopping. Perfect reciprocity is not achievable, since each side will see things differently and the exact balance will probably change over time, as day-to-day circumstances require some flexibility in your relationship rules.

Therefore, reciprocity in any given situation is not as important as *reciprocity over situations* or *reciprocity over time*. As will be discussed in the following chapters, conflicts can often be solved by creating new solutions that will meet both parties' needs. However, in some situations, it may still be impossible to get the balance just right. One way to overcome this is by trading benefits, favors, or sacrifices in certain situations or over periods of time. Some problems can be solved by exchanging privileges and responsibilities. For example, Susan agrees to take over paying the bills (a task that Tom despises) if Tom agrees to get up and make the first pot of coffee in the morning (a task that Susan finds almost impossible). Reciprocity over time involves an exchange between short-term and long-term benefits or sacrifices. Tom gives up his weekend to help Susan with a term paper in return for her undivided attention next weekend. In such exchanges, however, it is important to be sure that the short-term advantages aren't always received by the same person, since this can also create an imbalance of power.

Not surprisingly, research on marital satisfaction has repeatedly shown that couples who adopt a principle of reciprocity tend to report more satisfaction with their relationships than couples who do not. So, in general, reciprocity is the best policy.

Defining Sex Roles

Now, with the considerable change in men's and women's roles in society, it may be a good idea to think about how you wish to define sex roles within your relationship. Often, stereotypes about sex roles are at the basis of relationship conflicts, especially when partners have different ideas about what women or men "should" do or how they "should" be.

Rigid adherence to sex role stereotypes can cause couples to restrict their relationship and may even cut them off from pleasures that they might otherwise enjoy. For example, deciding that the male partner should initiate sex may cut both partners off from the considerable pleasure that other couples experience when the female shares this responsibility. Determining that it will be the woman's role to take care of the children and the housework may cut the male partner off from the pleasure of bathing his baby or reading to his children, or from the time he might have had with his wife had he done the laundry or cooked dinner. Deciding that the male should work and the female should stay home may deprive both of something they would enjoy more if they considered reversing their roles, working part-time, or making other arrangements for the daytime care of the children.

Of course, some couples are happy with the traditionally defined sex roles, and in such cases they should not try to conform to newly evolving roles any more than those who wish to try new types of relationships should be forced into the old mold. But be careful not to ignore this vital issue, for it is worth serious consideration. If different perceptions about sex roles are a source of some of your disputes, you may want to make them an early target for negotiation. Otherwise, they are likely to continue to haunt your everyday arguments.

Try to be sensitive to your partner's discontent with relationship rules, and consider the negotiation method discussed in the next few chapters to make readjustments when old rules are no longer satisfactory. Alterations to the power balance in your relationship will be an ongoing exercise. As with tuning a car, getting it right once doesn't mean that it will stay that way forever. Circumstances change and so do people. Regular tuning of your relationship, like your car, is the best way to keep it running smoothly.

5

Discovering Wise Ways to Win

Most of us have been well-indoctrinated in the idea that in a conflict situation, one side wins and one side loses. From years of watching television and movies, we have learned that it is the "good guys" who are supposed to win and the "bad guys" who are supposed to lose. Of course, we tend to identify with the good guys, who usually have good reasons for their behavior. The bad guys have either no reasons or bad ones. With all of this training, it is no wonder that we like to identify with the good guy who is right and deserves to win and label our partner as the bad guy who is wrong and deserves to lose.

Fiction seldom shows us conflicts where both sides have perfectly good reasons for wanting something different, making it difficult to tell the difference between the good guys and the bad guys. Further, we are rarely exposed to conflicts where both sides lose or both sides win. In fact, the good guy/bad guy premise makes it impossible, within the rules of drama, to have "lose-lose" or "win-win" solutions, since this would mean that good guys sometimes lose and bad guys sometimes win.

In real life, however, both sides can and usually do have perfectly legitimate reasons (especially from their own perspective) for wanting something different. And since real life conflicts are not constrained by the rules of drama, they can and do end in different ways. For example, one side may win and the other side may lose (a win-lose solution), both sides may lose (a lose-lose solution) or both sides may win (a win-win solution). Since these various outcomes affect the relationship and the probability of future conflict, it is important to know more about them.

Win-Lose Solutions Don't Last

The belief that conflicts naturally end with a winner and a loser is at the very root of the problem. People who think that this is the way the world works search for, and find, this kind of resolution. But since a win-lose solution meets only *one* party's needs, it does not really resolve the conflict. Although it may appear that a resolution has been reached, the victory is often short-lived, because the conflict between the partners' needs still exists. Usually, the partner who concedes will resume the dispute at a later time. Because winning often leads to this kind of reinitiation of the conflict, it has been called the "curse of winning." The unstable nature of the win-lose solution results in couples having the same arguments over and over, sometimes throughout the marriage. Hence, the amount of time devoted to conflict grows.

Not only are win-lose solutions temporary, but they may be the source of growing dissatisfaction in the partner who perceives him- or herself to be the loser. If both partners lose some of the battles, both may feel increasingly dissatisfied. Having one's needs brushed aside leads to a build-up of anger and resentment, which can ultimately undermine positive feelings. Thus, the result of a solution where one side concedes is growing discontent and endless conflict.

Lose-Lose Solutions Are Not Good for the Relationship

Conflicts can also end with solutions in which neither side wins; in fact, both lose. This is a common outcome and a distinctly unpleasant and frustrating one. In this case, both sides end up in a situation worse than before the dispute, even in the short term. Especially nasty or bitter arguments are likely to lead to this, since neither side has had its needs met. As a result, both partners will be motivated to reinitiate the conflict at a later time in another, usually unsuccessful, attempt to satisfy their needs. In addition, lose-lose solutions damage the relationship as both sides harbor intensifying feelings of anger and bitterness at the other's stubbornness. If this continues, separation or termination of the relationship is an extreme but common outcome.

Compromise Is Not the Best Solution

When partners are equally matched, conflicts can drag on until they end through sheer exhaustion. When it becomes clear that neither side is going to give in no matter how long the conflict continues, a stalemate is reached. Ironically, such situations can lead to a more adaptive phase of problem solving, where both parties finally realize that no matter what they do, they can't win. The stalemate forces them to abandon the goal of winning, to lower their aspirations, and to look for a compromise. Although a compromise is generally better than a win-lose or a lose-lose solution, often it is not the *best* outcome possible, since it means settling on a solution that only partially fills both parties' needs.

Win-Win Solutions: The Only Real Way to Resolve Conflict

The most satisfactory and stable solution is that in which both partners come out winners. Such win-win solutions occur when a resolution is found that meets both sides' needs. Unlike win-lose solutions, win-win solutions are lasting. Because both partners feel that a satisfactory answer has been found and their needs have been met, neither one is likely to reinstigate the conflict, and both are willing to adhere to the terms of their agreement. Moreover, the couple's overall level of conflict will be reduced, since the same battles do not have to be waged over and over again, and because every couple has only a finite number of issues over which they have conflict, the overall amount of conflict in the relationship will be dramatically reduced if win-win solutions can be found for even some of these. In addition, frustration and anger—the breeding ground of discontent—will be diminished.

Because partners have been taught that the natural outcome of a conflict is for one side to win and for the other side to lose, they often do not even consider the possibility that both sides *can* win.

There is a tendency to think of win-win solutions as an ideal that can only rarely be achieved. But in fact they can be found more often than partners imagine, if they know how to look for them.

The best way to find mutually satisfying solutions to conflicts of interest is for couples to learn how to negotiate on the basis of interests. There are basically two approaches to negotiation. One teaches people how to gain advantage over others and emerge as the victor. "Dirty tricks" are a regular feature of this method. This style of negotiation is sometimes taught to businesspeople for use in making deals, where the relationship is short-term, the aim of the negotiation is to get the better of the other person in a quick "hit and run" manner, and maintenance of the relationship is not important. In intimate partnerships such as marriage, however, such methods are extremely destructive. Hence, this type of negotiation is *not* recommended for use in intimate relationships.

The second approach to negotiation acknowledges the desire to win but also takes into account the importance of the relationship. The goal is for both parties to win so that the relationship itself can win. To accomplish this, a thorough assessment of each party's interests must be undertaken before a search for a solution is begun. When the assessment stage is completed, an active search for creative options is mounted, and these are then combined to build agreements that satisfy both sides' needs. Another important feature of this approach is learning to keep emotions under control, so that the first two activities don't get sidetracked into positional arguing or a fight about fighting.

Negotiating on the basis of interests requires partners to join in a mutual effort to tackle the problem, rather than each other. In this type of negotiation, they work together to find a solution. And by doing so, they form a "relationship about their relationship."

Negotiating on the basis of interests tends to work best if couples do it formally and follow certain steps in the process. The next several chapters will discuss in detail how to follow these steps. At first, some people feel uncomfortable with the idea of applying the plan formally (for example, writing lists of interests, as you will be instructed to do), and they are sometimes tempted to use it more informally instead. But that can often increase conflict and turn the negotiation process into a fight about fighting. Having a carefully designed plan for exactly how you will proceed is important in preventing conflict during negotiation.

The first step in any successful negotiation involves establishing the rules that will be used in the process. Sometimes negotiators take longer to agree to the rules than to negotiate the substantive issues themselves. For example, it was reported that negotiations over the shape of the table to be used at the Vietnam peace talks took years!

To minimize such problems, this book offers a plan based on the best negotiation methods available. Adhering strictly to it will help you to avoid unnecessary argument over the process and resultant fights about fighting. Instead, you will be able to concentrate your efforts on resolving the real conflict.

The following chapters will explain how you and your partner can begin the search for win-win solutions, which are, after all, the only wise way to win!

II

Basic
Negotiating

6

Turning Arguments
into Negotiations

It is very important to schedule regular times for negotiation. Regular sessions allow issues to be tackled when they first appear, before they grow into bigger problems. Such scheduling also ensures that no issue will go unresolved for long.

Another reason to establish regular times is that it is never a good idea to negotiate when you are angry. No matter how hard you try to engage in honest discussion, your anger is likely to spill over and convert the negotiation process into an argument. Having a regular time for your sessions makes it easier to keep arguments and negotiations separate, since issues that come up in the heat of an argument can be rescheduled for a time when the parties are able to talk about the issues more rationally.

How often you schedule sessions is up to you, but most people find that once a week is good. Extra ones can always be added if necessary.

When scheduling negotiations, it is best to plan them for times when you are likely to have privacy and little or no interruption. You may want to choose a period when the kids are away or asleep and when you are unlikely to have calls or visitors. In fact, you may want to take the telephone off the hook or simply not answer any calls. If possible, negotiation sessions should also be scheduled when you are both well rested, not particularly stressed, and when neither of you is under the influence of drugs, including alcohol. Weekends are often a good time. Decide on your schedule and do your best to stick to it. For example, it is better to agree to negotiate at a specific time—2:00 P.M. on Saturdays—than "sometime over the weekend." Sloppy planning can itself cause conflict, as each party waits for the other to initiate the session and feels disappointed and angry when the other fails to do so. You may find it equally upsetting if your partner wants to negotiate when you'd rather do something else. On the other hand, if you are the one who wants to negotiate when your partner doesn't, you may feel betrayed and hurt. Since the purpose of negotiating is to *prevent* unnecessary conflict, it is best to be specific in your planning.

When you have decided on a regular date and time, write it down, make arrangements to be free, and *stick to your plan*. If, for some truly unavoidable reason, you are unable to keep this commitment, suggest another time and do your utmost to be available then. The more you put it off, the more likely you are to experience your partner's anger in the session.

It is also wise to set a time limit for each negotiation session. An hour is a good length for most couples. Negotiating (without arguing) can be harder than you might imagine, so allow yourself enough time to make progress, but be careful not to become overly tired. If you have not finished negotiating, you can always arrange an additional session or hold the issue over until your next regularly scheduled one. If an issue comes up that can't wait, you can always schedule an ad hoc session, but be sure to wait until you are no longer angry.

When you first begin to negotiate, you may find that you have quite a number of unresolved or backlogged issues that require work. Whether you choose to tackle them in a concentrated manner or more slowly, you will probably need several sessions to deal with these problems. Over time, however, the process will speed up, as your negotiating skills increase. Moreover, you will find that once some of your initial problems have been worked out, the rest of your negotiations will be easier and less time-consuming.

So, a little patience and persistence is required. There are no quick fixes for relationship conflicts—there is only the challenge of learning how to listen to your partner, how to communicate your needs, and how to find creative solutions that will make you both happy.

How to Stop an Argument and Start Negotiation

Let's imagine that you're in the middle of a heated argument with your partner. Your partner is taking one position; you are taking another. The discussion is going nowhere and neither of you is winning. In fact, things are becoming more and more nasty, and you are beginning to feel attacked. *What can you do?*

What you can do (and this applies to either of you) is to simply stop the argument and put the topic on your agenda for negotiation. You could say something like this:

"Hang on a minute. We're both getting upset and arguing when we could be exploring our needs and concerns and considering some new options. I'd like to try to use the negotiation skills we have learned to see if we can find a mutually acceptable solution that would make us both happy. What do you say? Can we schedule a special negotiation session tonight at eight o'clock after the kids are in bed, to try to talk about it more rationally?"

Once you have agreed on a time, try to clarify the issue to be negotiated. Negotiation should always be about *future* behavior—not about past behavior. Issues that can be negotiated include how to divide up chores, what to do when one partner starts to feel jealous, how parents can be dealt with, or how money is to be spent. Issues that cannot be negotiated include who has been doing the most around the house, whether there was any cause to feel jealous, whose parents have been the most unreasonable, or who has been the most irresponsible with money. In other words, future behavior *can* be negotiated. Interpretations of the past *cannot*.

Continue working to identify the issue or issues until you both agree that they are important and that they involve future behavior. Once you have clarified what you will negotiate about, write it down so that you will remember exactly what it was.

Prepare for the Negotiation Session

All professional negotiators prepare for their work, and you may want to do so as well, by reading this book before you attempt your first session. You will need to have a good understanding of all of the steps before you proceed. To refresh your memory, a Skills Review section is presented at the end of the book. Also, since a negotiation session can turn into another argument if you don't manage emotions, it is a good idea to rehearse the skills discussed in chapters 11 and 12.

Work Together to Tackle the Problem

When the appointed time arrives, sit down on the *same* side of the table and place a piece of paper in front of you. Sitting across from each other (which is what people tend to do) puts you in an adversarial position, making it more likely that you will argue. Sitting on the same side of the table with the problem in front of you sets the tone for you to work collaboratively. As you proceed through the negotiation steps, write down the relevant information from each stage. Some couples may wish to buy a notebook just for this purpose. Couples who don't keep track of their progress tend to forget what they have accomplished, thus their negotiation sessions often become repetitive and they may overlook important interests. Incomplete notes can also be a source of conflict, so be sure to carefully record your progress.

Begin your negotiation by writing each of your names across the top of the paper, one on each side of the page. If you have already advocated positions, write each person's position below the name, as shown on page 61. Don't discuss your positions at this time. Just draw a line underneath them to separate each party's position from its interests. Now you are ready to begin negotiation with a thorough assessment of your partner's needs and concerns.

7

Understanding Your Partner's Needs and Concerns

It may seem odd to begin with your partner's interests rather than your own, since yours are probably uppermost in your mind. But beginning the negotiation process by exploring and carefully listening to your partner's needs and concerns will make your partner more willing to listen to you when it is your time to talk. If you are both reading this book, you may wish to establish a principle of fairness (such as tossing a coin) to decide whose interests will be discussed first.

It is best to discuss each person's interests one at a time. This allows each partner to thoroughly consider and discuss his or her own needs and concerns without interruption from the other person. Most people have never carefully considered their interests. Focusing on one person at a time allows that person to concentrate on the task. It also allows the partner who is listening to give undivided attention to the partner who is talking.

Ask About Needs and Wants, Fears and Concerns

What is meant by "interests"? Interests are what lie behind positions. They represent each person's needs, wants, fears, and concerns. They are the *real* issues that motivate the person's choice of a particular position. By understanding why a partner advocates a given position and what he or she really wants or is concerned about, it becomes possible to find ways to meet these needs that are acceptable to both parties. Thus, the first step is to understand your partner's needs and concerns by asking about them and then listening carefully to the answers. Sometimes people make the mistake of thinking that they already know their partners' interests, but, as you are likely to discover if you try this, you probably don't.

If the issue you are discussing is, for example, where you will go for your vacation, ask questions such as: "What do you want from our vacation?" "What do you feel you need from this vacation?" "What things about the vacation are important to you?" "Is there anything that worries or concerns you about our vacation?"

If your partner has already stated a position—for example, if your spouse has mentioned a specific place—ask *why* he or she wants to go there: "Why do you want to go to ———?" "What needs or wants would going to ——— satisfy?" "What worries or concerns do you have about doing something else?" "Are there any other reasons why this choice appeals to you?"

List Your Partner's Interests

As you proceed with your discussion, record your partner's interests on the side of the page under his or her name. (Your own interests will be recorded on the opposite side, during the next step of negotiation.) Writing down your partner's interests will help you to clarify them. Ask your partner to help you get the wording right. It is best to record interests in terms of wants, needs, fears, and concerns—for example, "wants to relax," "needs time away from work," or "concerned about the cost."

Listen Carefully to Your Partner's Interests

As your partner talks about his or her interests, *listen and don't interrupt except to ask clarifying questions.* Listening to your partner's interests is *not* the same as having a discussion. Discussion involves interactive conversation. In contrast, this exercise focuses on identifying your partner's interests as completely as possible, so that these can be taken into account when you brainstorm creative options later in the negotiation process. To do this properly, you will have to develop *active* listening skills.

Listening might seem easy, but it is extraordinarily difficult. There is a tendency to want to have your say as you go and to express your reactions to what your partner is saying. *It is essential to resist this temptation.* You'll have your turn later. Interjecting your interests now will only interrupt the flow of your partner's explanation and undermine your ability to genuinely hear and understand what your partner is telling you. Judging, evaluating, and criticizing your partner's interests should be scrupulously avoided.

Active listening means giving your partner your undivided attention. Look at your partner as he or she talks. If you are really listening, you cannot be doing anything else at the same time (such as fixing something, watching television, filing your nails, or pacing around the room). Provide nonverbal feedback when appropriate, such as nodding or smiling. Give your partner verbal encouragement with comments such as "Uh-huh," "I see," "Tell me more," "You're doing well," or "This seems like something important." If you need to ask questions to clarify something that you don't understand, try not to interrupt to do so. Rather, wait for your partner to pause.

Good listening not only means listening to the content but listening for meaning. A useful way to make sure that you understand your partner's perspective is to restate or reflect what your partner has said, using your own words. Although this may seem a tedious process, restating what you believe are the most important points will reassure your partner that you are listening and that you understand what is being said. Moreover, when you demonstrate that you care enough to listen, your partner will feel more comfortable about revealing deep-seated needs or concerns.

Some issues are difficult to talk about. You can help your partner explore these by listening for hints about these deeper feelings and then sensitively and gently probing for further information. Active listening helps partners clarify what they are feeling, and expressing feelings frequently makes people feel less fearful of them. Interests often are comprised of many layers. Some interests have deeper interests beneath them. If you don't fully understand an interest, or if you suspect there is more to it than your partner is stating, ask him or her what other needs or concerns might underlie the stated interest. It may be that your partner hasn't explored the area very carefully either, and this examination could lead to new revelations and greater understanding for both of you.

Some of the most important interests are basic human needs—to be loved, to experience recognition and acceptance, to feel important, to avoid failure, and to feel in control. Sometimes, these deeper needs are the most difficult ones to talk about, and revealing them can take real courage. Active listening to your partner can be of great help in getting him or her to open up and share these more important concerns.

What you should *not* do, however, is to guess or "mind read." Nothing is more annoying than someone who thinks he knows what you are thinking, especially when he is wrong! If you have a hunch about an interest that your partner has not mentioned, it is all right to ask whether you are right. But be sure to do it in a tentative way, and be careful not to belittle the interest or make it sound ridiculous. If your partner says that you are not right, don't argue! Just accept it. Remember, this is your *partner*'s view of his or her needs and concerns, not yours.

The purpose of active listening is to help you understand the other person's way of looking at the world. Active listening requires active receiving. To really listen, you have to suspend your thoughts and feelings and try to put yourself into your partner's reality. This is also called "empathetic listening," as your goal is to try to see the other person's "inner world" as if it were your own. In some cases, active or empathetic listening may cause you to change your attitudes and opinions about your partner. For example, you may find that it's harder to be angry at your partner when you understand how he or she feels.

As you listen to your partner, write down anything that seems to be a need or want as well as anything that sounds like a fear or concern. Your partner can work with you to make sure that the points you record are correct reflections of what was meant. Try to clarify the issues that you don't fully understand by asking more questions. Remember, however, not to talk about what *you* think or how *you* feel about your partner's needs or concerns. Just listen and clarify.

You may find that some of your partner's interests are contradictory. In fact, people frequently have conflicting interests, since issues are not always clear-cut. People experience conflict within themselves when their own wants, needs, or concerns are in conflict. If your partner's needs seem contradictory, just write them down as they are, without comment or criticism.

When trying to explain interests, people sometimes mistakenly mention a position. At times, it can be difficult to distinguish between a position and an interest. If you think that something your partner has mentioned is a position, say so, and work together to try to discover what interests might lie behind it.

When your partner has finished telling you his or her interests, try to summarize what was said. This is an important step because it verifies that you have understood correctly, and it assures your partner that you have listened actively. If you have misunderstood something, or if you only partly understood, ask your partner to explain in more detail until the information is clear to you. Finally, ask if there is anything else that hasn't been mentioned. For example: "Are there any other factors that are important to you in deciding where you'd like to go this year for our vacation?" If additional interests are forthcoming, add them to the list, and keep summarizing until both of you feel that you have a full grasp of your partner's interests.

Finally, it can also be helpful to validate what you have heard. This means letting the other person know that you think his or her interests make sense and are reasonable. It is not the same as agreeing, but it will make your partner feel accepted. This can be very therapeutic and in itself will go a long way toward meeting the very important basic need to feel accepted. Validation involves saying something like: "Your interests make sense to me and I think I understand them now. Some of my interests are different, but I accept that that is how you feel." For good measure, you can add: "I believe that if we're creative enough we might be able to find a way to satisfy both of our needs and concerns."

Susan and Tom's exploration of Tom's interests regarding their vacation plans is recorded below. Their written record of interests appears on page 61.

SUSAN: Are you ready to talk about your interests?

TOM: All set. Who's going to write them down?

SUSAN: I will, if that's okay. It'll help me understand them better. If I don't get it down right, you can correct me. Okay?

TOM: Fine.

SUSAN: All right. Why do you want to go to your parents' condo for our vacation this year?

TOM: I feel that my parents, especially mother, expects us to come.

SUSAN: (Resisting the urge to make a snide remark, probes further) What would concern you about that if we didn't go?

TOM: We'd have to put up with her getting angry at us, and you know what that's like. I've been working so hard that I don't think I could face it. Also, they're getting old and you never know how much longer they'll be around.

SUSAN: (Summarizing) So, you're concerned about trying to avoid upsetting your mother, and you feel an obligation to see them. Is that right?

TOM: Yes.

SUSAN: (Writes "Concerned about avoiding mother's anger" and pursues this line to develop a fuller understanding of this point) From your perspective, do you *want* to see them?

TOM: Not especially. It's just that I feel I *ought* to.

SUSAN: (Writes "Doesn't particularly want to see parents") I understand. Any other reasons you want to go there?

TOM: I like the beach.

SUSAN: (Probes further to see what the deeper interest might be) What is it about the beach that appeals to you?

TOM: The fishing's good—and you know how much I like fishing.

SUSAN: Yeah. (Writes "Wants to go fishing") Anything else?

TOM: It's cheap.

SUSAN: (Again resists the urge to comment and probes further, even though she thinks she already knows the answer; this avoids the danger of mind reading) Are you concerned about expenses?

TOM: Yes. I know you think I'm a cheapskate, but I don't want to dip in to our savings.

SUSAN: (Doesn't take the bait and writes "Concerned about the cost/doesn't want to use money in savings account") You'd prefer not to spend too much on our vacation. Is that right?

TOM: Yes.

SUSAN: Are there any other concerns you have about doing something different?

TOM: Well, just about anything else would require reservations, and I'm so busy at work I just don't want to hassle with all that.

SUSAN: Mm-hm. (Writes "Doesn't want to hassle with reservations") Any other concerns about doing something different?

TOM: Those are the main ones.

SUSAN: Good. Is there anything else you want from a vacation that we haven't covered?

TOM: What I really want is a chance to be with you and to get away from work and to relax.

SUSAN: (Smiles at Tom warmly) Great! (Writes "Wants to be with me, wants time away from work, wants to relax") Anything else?

TOM: That about sums it up.

SUSAN: Okay. I'll summarize what I've written and you can tell me whether I've got it all. If I understand, the reason you want to go to your parents' condo is that you feel an obligation to them, and even though you don't particularly want to see them, you're concerned that they might get angry, especially your mother. You also like going there because it's inexpensive and we don't have to touch our savings, and you can go fishing and relax, which you enjoy. You want to get away from work and spend some time with me, and because you are so busy right now, you don't want to be burdened with making reservations to go somewhere new. Did I hear you correctly? Is there anything I left out or got wrong?

TOM: That was good, but you didn't mention the bit about my parents getting old, and that's important. I'd feel terrible if we didn't see them and something happened.

SUSAN: (Reflecting) You're also worried that your parents are getting older and if one of them got sick or died, you'd feel terrible. Is that right?

TOM: Yes.

SUSAN: (Writes "Worried that something could happen to parents." Probes further to check out a hypothesis and avoid mind reading) Are you worried that upsetting them might make something happen to them?

TOM: No, I don't worry about that. I guess I'd just feel guilty if we didn't see them.

SUSAN: (Summarizing as she writes "Doesn't want to feel guilty") You don't want to feel guilty?

TOM: That sounds silly, doesn't it?

SUSAN: No. I understand.

TOM: It was good to talk about it. I appreciate it.

SUSAN: It was interesting for me, too. I feel that I understand you better.

Resist the Urge to Add Your Own Interpretation

Notice that Susan resisted all urges to sidetrack the conversation or to make her own points. Any issues that she didn't understand were clarified by further questioning. When she gave her summary, it was a straight restatement of Tom's points, with no embellishments, snide remarks, or interpretations. When you do this exercise with your partner, you should be absolutely scrupulous in resisting temptation to add provocative commentary or personal attacks (sometimes called "zingers") to your summary, even when you don't believe that your partner is telling the whole story. To illustrate the importance of this, imagine what would have ensued if Susan had added this interpretation to her summary:

SUSAN: You want to go to your parents' condominium again, even though we've been there the last five years, because you don't want to upset your precious mother, who always has to have her own way! I wish you cared as much about my feelings as you do about hers! Also, you say that you're keen to go fishing and to be with me, but how can you be with me if you go fishing? You know how much I hate it! You never consider my feelings. And I would hardly call staying with your parents "being with me"! You also say you're worried that going somewhere else would be too expensive. You worry about money

more than anyone I've ever known. Well, there's
more to life than money!

With this summary, Susan would never have discovered the
more intimate information that Tom later disclosed. Further,
having had his expectations and trust betrayed, Tom would
have been less willing to talk to her in the future.

So, keep your summary to a simple statement of what
you've written down and do *not* add anything to it. Continue
probing the major interests until both you and your partner
feel satisfied that they have been thoroughly investigated and
understood by both of you. After you summarize your partner's interests, ask for feedback until your partner agrees that
you have a clear understanding of his or her needs.

If partners abide by the negotiation steps, they are likely to
minimize or even avoid the more unpleasant and destructive
aspects of conflict. Sometimes, however, emotions or old
habits, such as blaming, can creep into the negotiation process; if not managed, these can destroy what has been
achieved. Chapters 11 and 12 discuss how to sidestep such
hazards and keep the negotiation process on track. Since emotions can become involved at any time during negotiation, it is
important to learn how to handle emotions before you sit
down to listen to your partner's interests.

Partners who tend to avoid conflict are often unaccustomed
to talking about needs and may be reluctant to start. In fact,
they may even have some trouble knowing what their needs
are, since they have been suppressing them for so long. Extra
patience, sensitive probing, empathetic listening, and practice
will be required to get the process under way. If the task is
still difficult, it may be useful to have a discussion about what
you can do to help your partner discover or disclose needs and
concerns.

Try to Understand How Your Partner Sees the Situation

One of the purposes of exploring your partner's interests is to understand how he or she sees the world. This is known as "perspective taking," because you are trying to see things from your partner's point of view. This can be a very enlightening experience. Your partner's perspective may suddenly make sense to you for the first time. Moreover, the very act of listening to your partner is likely to make you feel closer and more intimate, as your partner shares deeply felt desires, needs, and concerns. In addition, feeling that you care enough to listen may cause your partner to feel warmer toward you as well. Active listening is the first step in showing your partner that you *do* care about his or her needs.

Identifying the Most Important Interests

Having completed your list of your partner's interests, the final step in this phase is to identify the most important interests. Ask your partner to circle three or four of the most important ones on the list. Tom identified his most important interests as worry that something could happen to parents, not wanting to feel guilty about not seeing parents, wanting to be with Susan, and wanting to go fishing. Although you will want to use the complete list as the basis for brainstorming creative options, it is helpful to know which interests are most important, so that you can be certain that they are taken into account in the win-win solutions you devise later.

Once you've achieved the goal of active listening to and understanding your partner's interests, it's time to explore your interests.

8

Being Assertive About Your Needs and Concerns

Before you can tell your partner about your needs and concerns, you will have to determine exactly what they are. Most of us never stop to carefully examine the needs and concerns behind a particular position that we are advocating. Doing so can be an enlightening experience.

When it is your turn to consider your interests, begin by asking yourself the same sorts of questions as you asked your partner. For example: "What do I want or need from a vacation"; "What concerns do I have about a vacation?"; "Why do I want to go to _____?"; "What concerns would I have about doing something else?"

Explain Your Interests Without Provocative Commentary

When you explain your needs and concerns to your partner, try to express them as clearly and simply as possible. Don't forget to probe more deeply into any interests that seem to provide less than the whole answer. But remember that this is not an exercise in trying to *persuade* your partner about anything—you've been through that and it didn't work. Now, you are trying to communicate what you want or need and what you have concerns about. There will be time to consider *how* you can get what you need later in the negotiation process. This is also not the time to bring up old gripes or to engage in personal attacks. Rather, stick to the task at hand.

Ask your partner to write down your interests as succinctly as possible on your side of the page, opposite his or her list of interests. When all your concerns have been written, ask your partner to summarize. If he or she has not fully understood or has misperceived what you said, gently correct the misunderstanding by explaining in greater detail. Encourage your partner to resummarize until a full understanding has been reached. Messages are not always received with the meaning that was intended by the sender. Therefore, it is essential to be certain that you truly understand each other by summarizing what you thought you heard the other person say, and vice versa. This may seem tedious, but it is the only way to know that your communication has been heard as you intended it to be.

Susan's interests are shown on page 61. Note that while her interests seem straightforward, they are not the first things that she said. Gentle probing by Tom helped to flush them out. Their conversation went like this:

TOM: Your turn now. Why do you want to go to Mexico?

SUSAN: I don't know. I just want to get away from it all.

TOM: (Probes further) What do you mean by "get away from it all"?

SUSAN: Well, I guess I just want a break in our routine. And going to your parents' won't give me that.

TOM: (Writes "wants a break in the routine"; ignores the second, positional remark; asks for more information instead) What else does "getting away from it all" mean?

SUSAN: I feel that I need something new and different.

TOM: (Writes "wants a new and different experience") Is there anything special that you want from a new and different experience?

SUSAN: No, not really. I just want something different.

TOM: (Checking that what he's written is the whole story) Does "wants a new and different experience" cover it, or is there more about this that we should discuss?

SUSAN: No, that says it.

TOM: Are there any other needs or wants that going to Mexico would satisfy?

SUSAN: Well, I'd like to have some time alone with you, with no one else around, especially your parents. Your mother spends the whole time talking to me and it gets on my nerves.

TOM: (Resists the urge to become defensive and writes "wants time with me alone," then summarizes the second statement before writing it down to show that he's heard) And you don't want to have to listen to my mother talk, right?

SUSAN: You got it.

TOM: (Writes "doesn't want to listen to mother-in-law talk") Anything else? Any worries or concerns about doing something else?

SUSAN: Well, I don't want to have to do any housework—a vacation's not a vacation to me if I'm stuck doing housework.

TOM: (Again resists the urge to reply and writes "doesn't want to do housework") Okay . . . Anything else that you want out of a vacation?

SUSAN: I want to relax and to come back refreshed.

TOM: Shall we list that as one interest or as two?

SUSAN: Two.

TOM: (Writes "wants to relax" and "wants to come back refreshed") Anything else?

SUSAN: That's all I can think of right now.

TOM: Well, if you think of anything else, we can write it down later. Now I'll sum up what I heard you say about your needs and concerns.

SUSAN: Good.

TOM: (Looks at list in front of him) Let me see if I can get it right . . . What you want in a vacation is a chance to relax so that you can come back refreshed. You want to go somewhere new and different, somewhere that would provide a break in our routine, which you feel you need. You don't want to spend your vacation listening to my mother, and you'd like to have some time alone with me, instead. Is that right?

SUSAN: Not bad, but you forgot the housework bit.

TOM: Oh, that's right! And you don't want to have to do any housework.

SUSAN: Especially cooking.

TOM: (Adds "especially cooking" to "doesn't want to do housework" and restates what Susan has said to show that he has heard) Especially cooking.

SUSAN: That was good.

TOM: Thanks. I've got a better idea now about how you feel.

Compare this to the discussion on pages 11–12. As discussed earlier, Tom has not *agreed* to Susan's wishes by listening to them. How these interests are addressed will be worked out in the next stage of negotiation, and Susan knows that. But she feels better anyway, just knowing that Tom cares enough to listen to her feelings and even to ask about them in detail. Already the feeling between them has improved, which will make both of them more willing to work toward a mutually satisfying solution.

You probably noticed that although Susan was trying to explain her interests to Tom without provocative commentary, some subtle zingers occasionally slipped in. Tom, however, successfully kept the negotiation on track by ignoring them and maintaining his focus on active listening and trying to understand Susan's interests. By not taking the bait, he demonstrated his sincerity in wanting to hear about her interests. The anger behind Susan's occasional barbs was gradually defused by Tom's willingness to listen, without arguing or putting forward his own point of view.

As before, the next step is to identify the most important interests by circling them on the list. This ensures that they will be given sufficient attention when the search begins for ideas that can meet both sides' interests. As shown on the following pages, Susan identified her most important interests as "not wanting to listen to Tom's mother talk, not wanting to do housework—especially cooking, and wanting a new and different experience."

Once you have fully explored, communicated, and recorded your own interests, the next step is to compare them with those of your partner, to find where there is common ground.

TOM AND SUSAN'S LIST OF INTERESTS

Tom	Susan
Position: Wants to go to parents' condo for their vacation	*Position*: Wants to go to Mexico

Interests	Interests
Concerned with avoiding his mother's anger	Wants a break in the routine
Doesn't especially want to see his parents during vacation	Wants a new and different experience
Wants to go fishing	Wants time alone with Tom
Concerned about cost/doesn't want to use money in savings	Doesn't want to listen to mother-in-law talk
Doesn't want to make reservations	Doesn't want to do housework, especially cooking
Wants to be with Susan	Wants to relax
Wants time away from work	Wants to come back refreshed
Wants to relax	
Worried that something could happen to his parents	
Doesn't want to feel guilty about not seeing his parents	

TOM AND SUSAN'S LIST OF INTERESTS AND COMMON GROUND

Tom	**Susan**
Position: Wants to go to parents' condo for their vacation	*Position*: Wants to go to Mexico

Interests	Interests
Concerned with avoiding his mother's anger	Wants a break in the routine
Doesn't especially want to see his parents during vacation	Wants a new and different experience
Wants to go fishing	Wants time with Tom alone
Concerned about cost/doesn't want to use money in savings	Doesn't want to listen to mother-in-law talk
Doesn't want to make reservations	Doesn't want to do housework, especially cooking
Wants to be with Susan	Wants to relax
Wants time away from work	Wants to come back refreshed
Wants to relax	
Worried that something could happen to his parents	
Doesn't want to feel guilty about not seeing his parents	

9

Finding Common Ground and Brainstorming Creative Options

Now it is time to see what interests you have in common and where your differences lie. Examine your two lists of interests and draw lines between those that you share. When Susan and Tom did this (see page 62), they found that they both wanted to have a relaxing time and that neither really cared to see his parents, although Tom felt an obligation to do so. Also, both wanted to get away from work—Tom from his job, Susan from her housework. The rest of their interests, which are somewhat different, will serve as the starting point for the next step.

This very important stage of negotiation involves brainstorming creative options. Brainstorming is a method used to generate a wide range of new ideas. In negotiation, it is based on each party's list of interests. The ideas that arise are not meant to be solutions in and of themselves. Instead, the best ones will become the building blocks from which a potential win-win solution can be constructed.

The Rules of Brainstorming

The purpose of brainstorming is to open up new possibilities, and your job is to be as creative as possible. To facilitate this, *all* ideas, no matter how wild or crazy they seem, should be written down on a list. There will be time to evaluate them later. Wild ideas are encouraged because they can trigger other ideas that *are* useful. Lateral thinking involves thinking broadly.

A related rule is that no idea should be evaluated, criticized, or argued about at this stage. Censoring ideas does not promote creativity, which is the purpose of brainstorming. Thus, it's important to suspend judgment and to write all ideas *without* critical comment. This is hard to do, and both you and your partner may be tempted to criticize some of each other's ideas. If this happens, gently restate the no-criticizing rule. Sometimes people also censor their own ideas by thinking about why they won't work. The no-criticizing rule applies to your own ideas as well. There will be time to evaluate their feasibility later; right now, what you need is ideas—every one that you and your partner can think of.

Once these rules have been understood, you are ready to begin brainstorming. With the lists of interests in front of you, begin considering ideas that could meet these various wants, needs, and concerns. On another piece of paper, write down every idea that either of you mentions. Although it was important to take turns when discussing interests, brainstorming is, by contrast, a joint activity that you can do spontaneously. Both partners should participate in trying to come up with suggestions. Try to think of ways to meet your partner's interests as well as your own. Ideas may meet one or more interests. Don't worry about trying to find ideas that will meet them all. Also don't worry about being committed to ideas that you suggest, as you will have a chance to reject them later. So, be creative, and let the ideas flow!

Continue brainstorming until you have listed everything you can think of. It is not necessary to go through interests one at a time, as this can suppress creativity. However, at the end of the brainstorming session, be sure that you have considered creative options for each of the interests, so that no needs or concerns are overlooked. Keep working until you have a very long list of ideas and no new ones are forthcoming. Then try to think of additional ones. The more you search, the more likely you are to find some creative options that, when pieced together with other ideas, can be made into win-win solutions.

The first part of Susan and Tom's brainstorming is recorded below to give you an idea of how brainstorming can work. (See page 70 for the options that developed from this portion of their brainstorming.)

SUSAN: Are you ready to begin brainstorming? Let's put the lists of interests in front of us.

TOM: (Picks up a pen) Okay, where should we start?

SUSAN: Anywhere.

TOM: Well, what if we go to my parents' condo when they aren't there?

SUSAN: (Although she doesn't like this idea, Susan remembers the rules of brainstorming and refrains from commenting) Write it down on the list.

TOM: (Joking) We could hire a housekeeper so you wouldn't have to do any housework.

SUSAN: (Doesn't become defensive and returns the joke) Or you could do it all, including the cooking!

TOM: Yeah, but then you'd have to eat my lousy meals! What if we went to restaurants for all of our meals.

SUSAN: We're not supposed to reject any ideas—write both of those down.

TOM: Okay. (Writes them down)

SUSAN: Maybe we could invite your parents to come here another time, say Memorial Day weekend. . . .

TOM: That might work, especially if we made a point of doing something special when they came. (Records the suggestion)

SUSAN: I suppose we could even try to visit them more often during the rest of the year, if we didn't see them on our vacation. (Pauses) Maybe we should just leave the kids with them—sometimes I think that's who they really want to see anyway.

TOM: True. (Writes this down) I suppose I could ask Peter [Tom's brother] to check in on them, if we did that.

SUSAN: Yes, and we could call them often from wherever we were.

TOM: (Records these suggestions)

SUSAN: (Looking at the list and responding to Tom's concern about expense) We should think about going somewhere without having to use our savings. . . . I suppose we could stay someplace cheap.

TOM: Or we could camp . . .

SUSAN: Yuck!

TOM: No criticizing. (Writes down both ideas)

SUSAN: Oh yeah. Maybe we could persuade George and Ann to come with us so that we could share expenses.

TOM: (Forgetting the rules) I thought you said you wanted to be alone with me!

SUSAN: (Ignores the bait and keeps the brainstorming on track) No criticizing—we're supposed to be creative. Can you think of anyone else we could go with?

TOM: (Joking) My parents . . .

SUSAN: (Making a face) Write it down.

TOM: How about Mary and Jim?

SUSAN: Maybe George and Ann and Mary and Jim would all be interested.

TOM: (Writes this on the list)

SUSAN: Maybe we should think of some ways that we could get some extra money so that it's not such a big problem. . . . I suppose I could work overtime.

TOM: (Doesn't like this idea, but writes it down without criticizing) Maybe we should sell the boat. We're not using it anymore anyway. (Writes this down, too)

SUSAN: Or I could give up buying new clothes for a while.

TOM: (Is tempted to say something snide but refrains and instead writes it down) Is there anywhere else that you would find exotic or different enough to meet your need?

SUSAN: Sure, lots of places. I wouldn't mind going to New York, or to New Orleans . . . or Europe wouldn't be bad.

TOM: Hang on—I can't keep up with you. (Writes all of these down)

SUSAN: (Examining the list of Tom's interests) Maybe we should consider somewhere exotic where the fishing's good.

TOM: Now you're talking! I've heard that the Bahamas have good fishing.

SUSAN: (Smiling) Write it down. I suppose if we went to the Bahamas, we could even stop by your parents' condo on the way.

TOM: Yeah, to drop off the kids—after all, you did say you wanted to be alone with me. . . .

SUSAN: (Teasing) What about fishing?

TOM: (Smiling) A person can't fish all day!

Susan and Tom continued to discuss creative options even beyond the point of this emerging agreement. Sometimes, as happened here, the mere exploration of options based on both parties' needs will flush out a solution. At other times, the couple may have to go through a more formal stage of developing their options into win-win solutions, as discussed in the next chapter.

Notice that although Tom and Susan didn't always succeed in abiding by the rules of brainstorming, they both attempted to do so. By gentle reminders, they were able to help each other stay on track when the other person slipped up. It is also interesting to notice the change in the tone of the brainstorming as the exercise proceeded. Had Susan become upset with Tom's initial suggestion, they might never have realized that there was a range of other possibilities that they had not considered. Toward the end of the conversation, they began joining together to tackle the problem, instead of each other. The brainstorming stage allowed them to become joint problem solvers, working together to find an answer to a mutual problem.

Review the Options and Note the Most Promising Ones

When you are finished brainstorming, the next step is to review your list of creative options and circle the most promising ones. If either of you consider that an idea might be promising, it should be circled. Remember that you are not yet looking for solutions, but for options that, when modified and combined with other options, might provide a solution.

Page 70 shows the list of creative options that Susan and Tom came up with. Below is the beginning of the conversation they had when reviewing their options list.

TOM: (With list in front of him) Okay. Let's go through this again and decide which ones to circle. (Reading from the list) "Go to condo at a time when the parents aren't there." I'd like to circle that one as a possibility.

SUSAN: (Doesn't like this, but keeps quiet, remembering that it won't be included in the final solution if she doesn't want it to be) Okay.

TOM: "Hire a housekeeper." I meant that as a joke.

SUSAN: I sort of liked that one. . . .

TOM: Okay. (He circles it) What about "Tom does all of the housework, including cooking"?

SUSAN: I suppose it wouldn't be fair, although I'd enjoy it. Let's skip it.

TOM: "Go to restaurants for meals"?

SUSAN: That would help a little, I guess. . . . Okay, circle it for now.

TOM: (Reading from the list) "Go to Tom's parents for part of the time; do something different the rest of the time."

SUSAN: That's a possibility; let's at least circle it.

TOM: "See the parents another time." I'd like to circle that one—I think it has possibilities.

SUSAN: Yes, me too.

Susan and Tom proceeded in this way through the rest of the list of brainstormed options. Notice that they avoided arguing about which items should be circled by sticking to the rule of circling any item that either partner liked. Both were aware that they retained the right to veto suggestions during the next stage of the process.

Brainstorming can be a liberating experience when you begin to see that there are many ways to tackle every problem. In fact, by carefully considering a range of creative ideas, almost all couples can come up with win-win solutions. The following chapter teaches you how to do exactly that.

BRAINSTORMING IDEAS

Go to parents' condo when the parents aren't there
Hire a housekeeper
Tom does the housework—including the cooking
Go to restaurants for meals
See the parents another time, e.g. Memorial Day weekend
Do something special if parents come at another time
Visit parents more often throughout the year
Leave the children with parents and go away by ourselves
Make arrangements for Peter to check in on parents
Call parents frequently when on vacation
Stay in cheap accommodation
Camp
Invite George and Ann along to share expenses
Invite parents along but go somewhere new
Invite Mary and Jim
Invite George and Ann and Mary and Jim
Get more money . . . work overtime (Susan)
Sell the boat (Tom)
Forfeit buying new clothes (Susan)
Go somewhere else:
   New York
   New Orleans
   Europe
Go somewhere else with good fishing . . . Bahamas
Stop by parents on the way to the Bahamas
Drop off the kids
etc.

10

Building Win-Win Solutions

The final step in the negotiation process involves piecing options together into win-win solutions. The first part of this exercise requires you to form combinations of the creative ideas on your list, in an attempt literally to *construct* a solution with which both of you are satisfied.

As you begin to fit together different options, bear in mind that you are trying to address as many needs from each person's list of interests as possible—particularly those that were circled as the most important ones. You may find that additional options occur to you as you proceed. Your creativity will not stop with the completion of brainstorming, and it is good to be open to any new ideas that emerge during this stage.

Remember that more than one win-win solution may be possible. So, don't stop as soon as a promising one emerges. Keep going until you have exhausted your efforts and thought of every combination. Once you have arrived at several potential win-win solutions, you will need to decide which of them is the most promising. If you don't like a particular solution, be honest about it. Simply say: "I wouldn't be satisfied with that," or, "I don't feel that would be completely fair to me." Do not accept a solution that doesn't meet your major needs. Keep working on it until one is found!

Once you have arrived at what seems a mutually acceptable solution, ask: "Are we both happy with this solution? Do we consider it fair? Is it going to resolve our problem? Is it going to work?"

To give you the idea of how this building process works, part of the conversation between Susan and Tom is reproduced below. Their win-win solution is shown on page 79.

SUSAN: Well, maybe we should work with the idea of going to the Bahamas, since that one seems to have some mutual appeal.

TOM: It's true, I've always wanted to go fishing there. I read an article once about the big game fishing, and that's something I'd love to try—at least once! Would the Bahamas be new and different enough to meet your needs?

SUSAN: It would be just fine! The only reason I suggested Mexico is that Jan Tyler came back from there last year raving about it, but the Bahamas would be interesting too. But what about your parents?

TOM: Well, I liked your suggestion that we have them over at another time—before we go on vacation. I hadn't thought of that. Do you think it would be too much trouble?

SUSAN: Not if it means time without them later. If we did it over a holiday, like Memorial Day, it wouldn't be much trouble at all. What do you think?

TOM: That sounds fine, and we could plan something they'd enjoy—like a trip to Lake Brown.

SUSAN: The kids would like that too!

TOM: Speaking of the kids, do you think we could leave them with Mom and Dad when we go to the Bahamas?

SUSAN: Well, I'd miss them like mad, but it *would* be nice to have some time alone together—we haven't had that for years! Do you think your parents would mind?

TOM: My guess is that they'd love it.

SUSAN: How do you think the kids would react?

TOM: They like being at my folks' so much, they'd probably never even notice.

SUSAN: That would mean that we'd stop there both ways, so we could even see your parents—briefly.

TOM: That should satisfy them.

SUSAN: What about the expense? I can't see how we could go to the Bahamas cheaply.

TOM: Well, we could sell the boat—we haven't used it much lately.

SUSAN: But you used to really enjoy it. . . . What if I worked overtime instead?

TOM: I don't want you to do that. You're busy enough already. Besides, we don't have time for the boat anymore, and I'd like a vacation alone with you more.

SUSAN: Well, I can't say no to that! Let's look at our interests and see whether we've left out anything important. (Glances at Tom's list) What about your concern with avoiding your mother's anger?

TOM: Well, if we invite them here first, then see them both ways, and they get to have the kids all to themselves, *that* should satisfy them. If it doesn't, I'll have to practice our new negotiation method with them.

SUSAN: (Laughing) That would be a sight to see!

TOM: (Looking at Susan's list) The only problem with this
           solution is that you said you didn't want to listen to
           my mother talk, and if we dropped the kids off and
           picked them up again, we'd be there twice.

SUSAN: Well, if we didn't stay too long either time, and if
           you and I took turns listening, I could cope with that.
           Having the rest of the time alone with you sounds
           pretty good—relaxing on a beach all by ourselves
           sounds like heaven! (Looking at Tom's list once
           more) What about feeling guilty?

TOM: I'll ask Peter to check up on them, and we can al-
           ways call—we'll want to talk to the kids anyway.

SUSAN: When do we leave?

This may sound idealistic, but in fact, if couples have followed the steps of negotiation carefully, they often find that
this last step is a very positive experience. Negotiation on the
basis of interests works because both partners have considered the other's needs and have shown, in the process of active listening and taking the other's needs into consideration,
that they *do* care about each other enough to follow the negotiation steps. The positive feelings generated by these actions
increase throughout the process. Moreover, working together
to be creative—something that couples usually don't do—can
also lead to a new sense of optimism and hope. Partners may
suddenly come to see that they don't have to be endlessly
locked in battle, and that maybe they can get along after all.

Of course, not all final stages of negotiation go this
smoothly. Some problems are harder to resolve than others.
Moreover, couples sometimes find it difficult to follow the
negotiation steps without resorting to an argument. Chapters
11 and 12 discuss ways to keep negotiations from turning
back into arguments.

What If a Win-Win Solution Isn't Found?

If you cannot find a win-win solution, consider returning to the early steps of negotiation and going through the process again. Encourage your partner with a positive suggestion, such as: "Let's try again—there must be a way to solve this!" Just because you haven't found the right solution doesn't mean that there isn't one. However, it may be a good idea to take a break before you try again.

Often, a win-win solution is not reached because one or more important interests were not discovered (or disclosed) and consequently were not addressed. Deeply rooted interests or hidden agendas can cause such an impasse. Therefore, a re-examination of each partner's interests is a good idea. Explore your own interests to be sure that you have fully disclosed them and ask your partner to do the same. Ask yourselves: "Is there anything else bothering us that we haven't brought up?" You may both discover interests that you were unaware of.

Partners who adopt avoidant styles and are out of touch with their feelings may need to work especially hard to discover the full range of their interests. Men may have a more difficult time with this task than women, since they are usually socialized to believe that they "shouldn't" have needs or fears. If this is the case with your partner, you might remind him that having wants, needs, fears, and concerns is *normal*, and that sharing them with you will be likely to strengthen your mutual understanding and trust. So, if you haven't reached a satisfactory solution, go a little deeper and try again.

Brainstorming is another process to repeat. There are endless possibilities in this area, limited only by your imagination. Often, a second attempt at brainstorming (after a break) will yield new creative options that can be pieced together to create a solution that will satisfy you both. Finally, if emotions get in the way, as they are particularly apt to do with some topics, try to follow the suggestions in chapters 11 and 12.

Two other strategies for developing win-win solutions involve dividing the problem into smaller components, and expanding the problem. In the case of dividing the problem into smaller components, if Susan and Tom had not been able to come up with a win-win solution, they could have considered dividing the vacation into smaller segments and negotiating about these. Thus, instead of negotiating where they would go for the entire vacation, they could have negotiated different solutions for each week. Expanding the area to be negotiated, or "expanding the pie" as it is called in negotiation jargon, can also work. In this case, instead of considering this year's vacation by itself, Susan and Tom could have included the next two years' vacations. So, if you don't find your solution immediately, keep trying, and remember that no problem is too big to solve if you explore it thoroughly, then break it into smaller problems or view it in a larger framework.

Develop Your Solution Further

Once you have achieved the basis for a win-win solution, continue to develop your plan until it is genuinely appealing to both of you. Ask your partner how the current plan could be improved upon: "What would make it better?" or "What would make it more attractive?" When Susan asked this of Tom, he revealed that his holiday would be complete if she would join him (even if she didn't want to fish) for a day of deep-sea fishing. When Tom asked Susan the same question, he discovered that her fantasies involved romantic dinners under swaying palms. When these "wants" were added to the plan, it became even more attractive to both parties.

Plan Who Will Do What by When

As shown on page 79, when a win-win solution is found, the two parties can go on to discuss how it will be implemented and to make some agreements about who will do what by when. It is a good idea to record these decisions and to plan another time to discuss progress. Many negotiations go astray at this point, and failure to be specific in plans to implement the solution can be the cause of unnecessary conflict. So, decide who will do what by when and keep a record. Then sit down together at an appointed time to discuss both partners' progress toward their assigned goals. Here is a brief excerpt from Susan and Tom's discussion:

SUSAN: Well, what do we do about planning who does what by when? (Pauses) I guess I could call up the travel agent tomorrow and ask about the cost of airfares and hotels and also see about availability—since you don't have time to hassle with reservations right now.

TOM: That sounds good. Once you've done that, I'll write to my parents and see how they feel about keeping the kids and about coming up for Memorial Day weekend. I'll try to do that by the end of the week. Okay?

SUSAN: (Nods) But before we do any of that, I'd like to talk it over with the kids to make sure they agree.

TOM: Right. When should we do that? Tonight after dinner?

SUSAN: Good. I'll write all of this down. Is there anything else we need to do?

TOM: Well, I'll put an ad in the paper for the boat. I can do that tomorrow.

SUSAN: Anything else?

TOM: I'll talk to Peter after we've sorted things out with Mom and Dad.

SUSAN: When should we review all this?

TOM: How about if we spend part of our usual negotiation time on it next week?

SUSAN: Fine. How about a cup of coffee to celebrate?

TOM: Great!

In most cases, such plans need little enforcement. If you and your partner have achieved a genuine win-win solution, your commitment and motivation to follow through on implementation of the plan is not likely to be a problem, since doing so will be in your own self-interest. However, if it does become a problem for either partner, it is better to express disappointment than to blame or get angry.

There are several common reasons why partners don't carry out the agreements they have made: Forgetfulness may cause problems, the task may be too difficult, or your partner may have agreed without really meaning it. Finally, your partner may be testing to see whether *you* will stick to the agreement!

If your spouse has simply forgotten, your expression of disappointment is likely to work better than a reminder, which will sound like nagging. If the task is too difficult or if your partner agreed without really meaning it, you will need to re-open the negotiation to find another way to resolve the problem. If your partner is testing to see if you will stick to the agreement, the best thing you can do is to pass the test by continuing to do what you agreed to. Once convinced that you are going to live up to the deal, your partner will come around and do his or her part. However, testing can go wrong when partners don't recognize that the other person's inaction is just that—a test. Instead, they interpret it as proof that their problems are insoluble, and this can precipitate a still greater problem. So, again—if your partner hasn't done his or her part, express your disappointment and stick to your side of the bargain. Chances are that your partner will respond positively. If not, you will have to return to the negotiation table.

The search for win-win solutions can bring couples closer together as the wisdom of each is mobilized in the search for a solution. If you are to succeed at this goal, however, one additional set of skills is needed: the ability to handle emotions—both yours and your partner's.

Susan and Tom's Win-Win Solution

Invite Tom's parents to our house for Memorial Day weekend and take them to Lake Brown. Go to the Bahamas for our vacation—just the two of us, without the kids. Stop by Tom's parents' condo (briefly) on the way there and on the way back to drop off and pick up the kids. Ask Peter to be in touch with Mom and Dad while we are away. Call Mom, Dad, and the kids from the Bahamas to check in with them. Sell the boat to raise extra money for the trip.

To improve the solution further: When in the Bahamas, Susan will go deep-sea fishing with Tom, and Tom will participate in romantic dinners.

WHO WILL DO WHAT BY WHEN

1. Talk to the kids about the plans.
   Who? Both of us
   When? Tonight after dinner
2. Call the travel agent to ask about airfares and hotels.
   Who? Susan
   When? Tomorrow

3. Write to Tom's parents (a) to tell them about the plan, (b) to see whether they would be willing to keep the kids, and (c) to invite them here for the Memorial Day weekend.
   Who? Tom
   When? By this weekend
4. Find out how to put an ad in the newspaper
   Who? Tom
   When? Tomorrow
5. Talk to Peter about looking after the parents.
   Who? Tom
   When? After the parents reply
6. Review progress.
   Who? Both of us
   When? At next week's regular negotiation session

11

Managing Your Own Emotions

Handling emotions in a conflict situation is not easy for anyone. When partners are in conflict, they feel angry and want to act out that anger.

Anger Can Turn Negotiating Back into Arguing

Managing emotions is one of the hardest but most important tasks in negotiating, since emotions can hinder problem solving and in fact derail the entire negotiation process. The negotiation methods outlined in this book are designed to minimize negative emotions, but feelings of anger or tension may still occur, especially when couples are discussing "hot" issues that have been argued about in the past and about which there are still strong feelings.

Although emotions can become involved at any stage of the negotiation process, there are three points that are particularly risky. The first is when your partner is discussing his or her needs and you are trying to listen. Listening to your partner's concerns while not mentioning your own can be difficult, as you may feel that you are being asked to suppress or ignore your own needs. It is even harder when people mistakenly believe that listening implies agreement. The second point where emotions are likely to interfere is when you are discussing your own needs. You may be tempted to dredge up previous instances when your needs were frustrated or ignored. The third high-risk time is during brainstorming, when your partner suggests an idea that you do not like. Some people fear that writing down an option that they don't agree with will mean that they have to accept it. One useful strategy is to remember that the entire negotiation is designed to allow both partners to have their needs met, and that you will have complete say over what is included in the final win-win solution and complete control over whether you want to agree to it.

Anger Comes from Hurt

Since anger is a common emotion during conflict, it is useful to know something about it. The most important thing to understand is that it is a secondary emotion that occurs in response to some other emotion. Usually, anger occurs in response to feeling hurt. When partners perceive that their needs are being ignored, they tend to make certain interpretations about why this is happening. One of the most common is that their partners do not care enough to meet, or even understand, their needs. This thought makes them feel hurt, which in turn can cause them to feel angry.

Contrary to common wisdom, emotions do not just occur automatically in response to situations or events. Instead, they occur in response to what people tell themselves about certain situations. Thus, how we *think* about a given event affects how we feel about it, and how we feel about it can lead to how we behave. Consequently, hurt and angry thoughts can lead to hurt and angry feelings, and these may lead to angry behavior.

When people are angry, they engage in a familiar host of behaviors. They raise their voices, say blaming and nasty things, or call each other names. Or they may punish each other by cutting off communication: They walk away, clam up, or refuse to discuss the issue. Whether couples adopt blaming styles or avoidant ones, angry behavior is self-defeating. It doesn't get them what they want! Rather, angry behavior makes it *less* likely that their needs will be met, since it causes the partner to become angry in turn and therefore even less responsive to their needs. Moreover, angry behavior makes it difficult for the spouse to recognize the hurt behind the anger.

The diagram on page 84 shows the sequence of events, interpretations, emotions, and responses that led Tom to become angry with Susan. Tom's anger began with his belief that Susan was ignoring his needs and with his interpretation that "she doesn't care." This thought left Tom feeling hurt. Then he began to review all of the other times that Susan had had her own way. The more he thought about it, and about all the things that he had done for her, the more angry he felt. His conclusion, that Susan was acting unfairly, further escalated his anger. Then, instead of telling Susan about his unmet needs or his feelings of hurt, he acted out the anger by accusing her of being "selfish," hoping that she would see that he was upset and would do something to remedy the situation. But his accusation only enraged Susan, causing her to respond with a counteraccusation that it was Tom who was selfish. In addition, Tom's angry attack made Susan less concerned about meeting his needs.

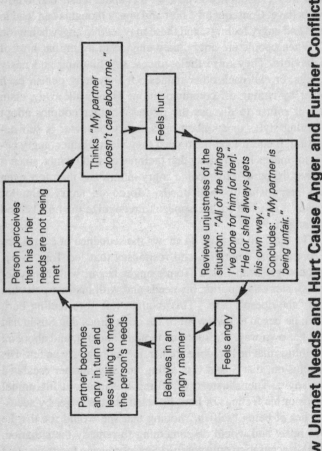

How Unmet Needs and Hurt Cause Anger and Further Conflict

Instead of achieving what he wanted, Tom's angry behavior merely interfered with Susan's ability to decipher his message. Moreover, Susan's counterattack convinced Tom more than ever that she didn't care. In the end, he felt even more hurt and angry—and so did she.

Of course, not everybody has precisely the same thought as Tom had, but the cycle is a common one, with minor variations on a theme. In short, angry behavior is not an effective way to ask your partner for what you want.

Expressing your needs more directly will be discussed in chapter 15. Fortunately, however, there are a number of other strategies that can be used to manage emotions. The next time you begin to feel overly emotional, you may want to try using them. If one doesn't work, try another. In some cases, you will need a combination of strategies to overcome your emotions.

Consider Alternative Interpretations

What makes us upset is how we interpret situations or events, rather than the events themselves, so a good place to begin is by changing our interpretations of events. All of us engage in a kind of internal dialogue called "self-talk." By changing how we talk to ourselves, we can actually change how we feel.

If, instead of assuming that Susan's inattention meant that she didn't care, Tom had interpreted her behavior to mean that she was preoccupied with worry about their daughter's poor school performance, he might have felt more empathetic and have offered to help, rather than become angry. An offer of help would probably have been welcomed, and would likely have caused Susan to feel more responsive to Tom's needs when he did express them.

As mentioned earlier, because partners are aware of the circumstances that influence their own behavior but unaware of those that influence the partner, they generally assume that the partner's behavior is due either to some undesirable personality characteristic or to the "fact" that the partner no longer cares about them. For example, Tom may excuse himself for losing his temper because he was "tired," but he may believe that the reason Susan lost hers was because she is "ill tempered" and doesn't love him anymore! When Tom forgot Susan's birthday, Susan decided that this was proof of Tom's "inconsiderateness." This, she decided further, was conclusive proof that Tom no longer loved her. To support this theory, she began to review all the other times that he had been inconsiderate, such as last week when he came home late without calling, yesterday when he forgot to pick up the dry cleaning, two years ago when he took the kids skiing even though she was sick, the times when they were first married when he used to "roll over" and fall asleep after making love. . . . Generalizing in this way doesn't get at the cause of your partner's behavior—it only makes matters worse, since it compounds your anger and causes you to believe that there is nothing more to understand.

What can you do instead? Let's imagine that you begin to feel more and more angry. What can you do about it? One thing is to try to understand the situation from your partner's point of view. To do this, consider (or even write down) how your partner would describe the situation, what he or she might be thinking and feeling. In fact, it is often the case that your partner is doing exactly the same thing as you are—thinking that you don't care, feeling hurt, reviewing how unfair and unjust your behavior is, and feeling angry with you for your lack of consideration. Your spouse may be remembering all the times when you had *your* way and thinking about all the things that he or she has done for you!

Trying to understand what your partner is thinking or feeling is an important first step in understanding the reality of the situation. You will feel differently when you realize that your partner has the same fears as you have. The bottom line is likely to be that both of you want to know that the other person *does* care. Fortunately, the negotiation method is designed to make this possible. If you carefully follow the negotiation steps, you will go a long way toward alleviating your partner's fears, and you may end up feeling less hurt and angry yourself.

One way to understand the circumstances that may have led to your partner's actions is to engage in "perspective-taking." This means putting yourself in your partner's shoes to see things from his or her point of view. A good way to do this is to imagine that you *are* your partner. Once you have adopted this role, try to figure out what your reasons are for acting this way and what circumstances are affecting your behavior. When Susan engaged in perspective-taking to understand why Tom had forgotten her birthday, she remembered that he had been working on an important submission for a board meeting and that he had been very tired lately. When she realized that he hadn't had a day off for five weeks and that he was forgetting lots of things that he normally remembered (like the dry cleaning), she started to feel less angry and more sympathetic. And when she thought about how embarrassed and upset he would be when he discovered his mistake, she felt even more sorry for him!

Taking your partner's perspective is one of the most important aspects of successful negotiating. If you are able to do this, you will be well on the road to a more satisfying relationship. Chapter 14 is devoted to a more detailed discussion of this important subject.

Use Calming Self-Talk When You Feel Emotional

Often, people mull over hurtful or angry thoughts, reviewing what the other person said or what they would like to have said or done. Usually, this only makes them more angry. A better strategy is to replace angry self-talk with calming self-talk. Substituting calming thoughts for angry ones can have a powerful effect on how you feel.

Calming self-talk means (silently) saying to yourself things like, "Just stay calm"; "Relax. Don't get upset"; "It's okay"; "Don't get angry"; "Just let it pass"; "It doesn't matter"; "Take it easy"; "Don't let him/her upset you"; and so on. This kind of self-talk is known as "self-instruction" since you are actually instructing yourself in how to behave.

If you practice calming self-talk, you will find that it can have amazing effects. Sometimes, however, people find it hard to remember to use calming self-talk when they are at their angriest. For this reason, it is a good idea to practice whenever you are feeling even mildly upset. You may also want to identify some sort of cue that will help you remember to use this strategy at more difficult times. The best cues are the early signs of your anger. Anger is easiest to control *before* it becomes intense. A physical cue, like the tightening of your stomach or the clenching of your teeth, can help you to recognize that you are beginning to feel angry. Angry thoughts can also serve as a cue. It is time to begin practicing your calming self-talk when you first notice angry thoughts. The idea is a simple one—just start talking to yourself in a calming way. Tell yourself:

> It's okay. Just stay calm. Relax. Take it nice and easy. Just try to stay relaxed . . . Good, that's it. Just keep relaxing. Don't let yourself get upset. Just stay nice and calm . . . Don't raise your voice. That's it, you're doing fine.

If you can keep this up whenever you begin to feel tense, you will find that, when added to the following suggestions, it *is* possible to control your anger.

Use Calming Self-Talk Before You Feel Emotional

Of course, another very useful approach is to practice calming self-talk *before* you become angry. To do this most effectively, you will have to identify high-risk situations. Since negotiation involves dealing with topics that have a history of being contentious, it is useful to practice calming self-talk in preparation for negotiation. Self-talk can help you stay in a rational, problem-solving mode and avoid negative emotions. All you have to do is silently tell yourself:

> All right, now I'm going to try to remember to use calming self-talk whenever I begin to feel angry or tense. I'll try to stay calm and relaxed and cool. If I find myself getting tense, I'll take a couple of deep breaths and pause for a moment. When I do talk, I'll try to keep my voice down and speak slowly. I think I can do it, if I just remember what I have to do.

Act Calm, Feel Calm

Acting calm can also help you to stay calm. The corollary can also be true: Acting angry can make you feel angry. Thus, it is important to try to act in a calm manner, even when you do not feel calm. Try to keep your voice at an even pitch. Speak slowly and calmly. You will find that simply slowing down will have a positive effect on how you feel and on your partner's response.

Since it is impossible to feel angry and relaxed at the same time, try to relax. Take a few deep breaths. Let your body go limp. Try to identify tense areas of your body and relax them. If your stomach feels tense, let go of the tension. If your neck is tense, make a conscious effort to relax your neck muscles. Imagining a relaxing scene can be useful as well. For example, imagine that you are lying on a beach and listening to the sound of the surf, or that you are lying at the top of a grassy hill, feeling the warmth of the sun on your skin.

Explain How You Feel and Why

If your emotions get out of control, resist the urge to engage in unfair fighting tactics. Some of the most common ones include personal insults, name calling, saying "you always" or "you never," and rehashing old grievances. (Chapter 16 will discuss these further.) Also be careful not to use dogmatic or accusatory wording. Try to use less inflammatory phrases instead, such as, "it seems to me," or "I think," or "it feels like . . ."

To reestablish control, speak assertively, honestly expressing how you feel, but in a way that doesn't attack your partner. The best way to do this is to explain how you are feeling and why. For example, you can say: "I'm feeling upset because I'm feeling personally attacked." This is useful for two reasons. First, it allows you to get your emotions out into the open: second, it gives your partner insight into how you are reacting and why. Explaining why you are upset is not provocative, and it causes your partner to see things from your perspective and realize that you *are* feeling hurt and unfairly treated.

Some people have trouble describing their feelings. The chart on page 92 can be used to help you think of the word that most accurately describes how you feel.

Take "Time Out" to Regain Your Perspective

Time out from negotiation is another strategy that can be used to reestablish control over your emotions. Getting away from the conflict situation can allow you to calm down and regain your perspective. Forcing discussion when you are very angry will lead only to words or behaviors that you may later regret. Time out is helpful, however, only when it is used constructively. Constructive use of time out requires explaining to your partner that you want a break from the negotiation in order to calm down and get your emotions back under control. A time to resume negotiating should be scheduled for the not-too-distant future, and it is essential that you return to the negotiation when scheduled.

Unfortunately, some people use time out destructively, to punish the other person, as when one spouse walks out of the room or leaves the house. It is important that you do not use time out in a punitive manner, since that will serve only to escalate the conflict.

Time out can also provide an excellent opportunity to reflect on both your own and your partner's interests, as well as new creative options, so that when you return to negotiating you will have some new insights and ideas. This may help you and your partner to achieve a win-win solution. Remember that focusing on problem solving rather than on blaming is the key to getting derailed negotiations back on track.

FEELINGS CHART

Positive

satisfied	curious	sentimental
receptive	tender	affectionate
relaxed	secure	peaceful
calm	strong	confident
glowing	happy	interested
warm	pleased	turned on
sexy	content	ambitious
excited	loving	imaginative
willing	fortunate	close-to-you

I feel ← a little
    ← somewhat
    ← very

Negative

grouchy	alone	frustrated
sad	trapped	sorry
anxious	put down	incompetent
tired	silly	rebellious
nervous	shy	confused
ashamed	hurt	listless
bored	guilty	depressed
grumpy	upset	embarrassed
annoyed	irritated	angry
tense	impatient	temperamental

(Adapted from Gottman, Notarius, Gonso and Markman, *A Couple's Guide to Communication*, 1976)

Let Go of Your Anger

If you decide to use time out to reestablish control over your emotions, there are several things that you can do to rid yourself of angry feelings. First, time itself has a way of easing anger. Energetic physical activity, such as jogging, swimming, or other vigorous exercise, can also help. If you have had relaxation training or know how to meditate, this is a good time to practice these skills. Listening to soothing music can also be helpful. Finally, humor can make you feel better, so you may wish to consider doing something that will make you laugh.

Before you resume negotiating, check out whether you are both feeling calm. If you are, then go ahead. If not, arrange a further period of time out and another appointment to resume negotiation.

Seek Additional Help If Anger Is a Serious Problem

This chapter has addressed how you can have a more constructive response to your emotions, especially anger, if they occur during the negotiation process. Some people, however, have special problems with managing anger. Often this is because they grew up in homes where anger was managed destructively. As a result, they never learned how to handle it any other way. In other words, they have observed many examples of how to be angry destructively, but they have learned little or nothing about how to manage anger constructively. Chapter 19 discusses what to do if destructive anger leads to violent behavior between you and your spouse.

Anger Is Not a Good Way to Get What You Want

Some people believe that acting out their anger is a good thing because it is "cathartic." Those who advocate such catharsis believe that bottling up anger causes it to get worse and that the only real way to get rid of it is to "let it out." But, on the contrary, expressing anger makes some individuals feel even more angry. And even when venting anger does work to make the person feel better, it almost always makes the general situation worse, since it typically results in counteraggression. The person who has vented his or her anger may feel better for a few seconds, but the ensuing counterattack usually erases the short-term gains. Angry exchanges like this usually end in shouting matches that exacerbate, rather than resolve, the conflict.

A much better way to deal with anger is to use skills such as negotiation, listening, and assertion to meet your needs. When angry feelings do crop up, you can choose to express them constructively, and you can control how long you will allow your anger to last. Choosing to use methods that will be effective in meeting your needs is far more satisfying than letting your anger rise out of control. Remember—anger is not a good way to get what you want. Using the negotiation method is!

If you can manage your emotions and keep the negotiation on target, praise yourself for the accomplishment. It is the hardest part of learning to negotiate, and it requires considerable practice if you are to become good at it. However, if you succeed even in a small way, you still have a right to feel proud. Learning to handle your emotions can be one of the most challenging tasks of your adult life. It is the ultimate step in accepting responsibility and gaining control over your happiness.

12

Handling Your Partner's Emotions

An important part of learning how to handle your emotions involves learning how to handle your partner's emotions. There is probably nothing that will incite you to anger faster than your partner's anger—when it is directed at you! If you are to remain calm and rational and to keep the negotiation on track, you will have to learn how to handle your partner's emotional outbursts as well as your own.

As discussed in the preceding chapter, engaging in a counterattack is *not* productive and will prevent you from reaching your goal. The best ways to manage your partner's emotions involve sidestepping angry outbursts, addressing feelings of hurt, and returning to the negotiation process. The following suggestions are aimed at doing just that.

Don't Respond

When your partner goes on the attack, simply don't respond. Instead, listen quietly. Let your partner continue until he or she has run out of steam. Ask questions to clarify anything you don't understand. Then quietly summarize what your partner has just told you, including how he or she is feeling. For example, you might say: "It sounds as if you're feeling really furious at me because you feel that I didn't listen to what you said. Is that right?" or, "You are saying that it really irritates you when I go ahead and do things without consulting you. Is that right?" The formula for this type of statement is: "It sounds as if you are feeling ———— because of ————. Is that right?"

Summarizing your partner's feelings and the rationale behind them demonstrates not only that you have listened and heard, but that you have understood why your partner is feeling that way. Showing that you have listened is not an admission that you were wrong! You are *not* agreeing that your behavior should be interpreted in a certain way or that you intended your behavior to mean whatever your partner has construed it to mean. You are merely acknowledging that you understand that this is how your partner sees the situation.

Not responding when your partner becomes emotional or attacks you will be exceedingly difficult. But it will have a powerful effect in diffusing volatile situations.

Don't Counterattack

Another important thing to remember is not to respond in kind to personal attacks or "zingers." Personal attacks come in many forms, including accusations, insults, name calling, insinuations, and interpretations of your behavior that put you in a bad light. If your partner attacks you in any of these ways, ignore it! Instead of taking the bait, simply sidestep the attack. Ignore the part of the message that was intended to wound you.

It may seem that remaining quiet would invite further attack, but instead it usually causes the other person to soften the attack or to restate the grievance in a less offensive way. The "argument game" is characterized by attack and counterattack, but nobody wants to feel that he or she is the aggressor. If one side refuses to play the game by refraining from counterattack, the other party will have to stop as well, otherwise he or she will appear to be the villain. In other words, if you change the game, your partner will *have* to respond. This is a game that can't be played for long without a partner!

Your task, then, is to *refuse* to argue. This is not the same as refusing to discuss the issue. You should maintain a willingness to return to negotiation at any time. Using calming self-talk as discussed in the preceding chapter can help. For example, during a negotiation session about disciplining the children, Susan found self-talk helpful when Tom launched into complaints about her "leniency." Susan used the following self-talk:

> Just ignore this. Don't get uptight. Don't respond.
> Just listen. Don't let this get to you. Remember,
> Tom is doing this because he feels unfairly treated.
> Just keep your cool! Don't attack back! Try to re-
> member to summarize what he has said. Focus on
> how he sees it. How is he feeling? Why is he feeling
> that way?

Susan let Tom complain until he ran out of steam, then she summarized how she thought he was feeling and why. As calmly as she could, she said: "You're angry at me because you think I let the kids off the hook when you've asked them to do something. Is that right?" This statement caused Tom to feel that Susan *had* heard his concerns and left him feeling more willing to return to negotiation.

Don't Defend Yourself

Although it can be even more difficult, it is essential that you also resist the urge to defend yourself. The problem with defending yourself is that it tends to sound as though you are rejecting or devaluing your partner's point of view. This usually leads to another round of both sides trying to convince the other that their perspective is the *right* one. Because neither partner feels listened to, each increases his or her attempts to be heard, and consequently both become more insistent and argumentative.

As mentioned earlier, listening first, rather than insisting on being listened to, can make your partner feel heard and cause him or her to be more willing to listen to you in return. Even more important, it can rid you of the anger and the "tit for tat" exchanges that can derail the negotiation process. Handling your partner's anger by listening to and acknowledging his or her feelings can help you to bring the negotiation back on track.

Address Your Partner's Sense of
Injustice and Hurt

Sidestepping your partner's anger and addressing the sense of injustice or hurt that lies behind it can work wonders in defusing emotional outbursts. Sometimes a simple gesture, such as taking your partner's hand, or giving your partner a hug, will be effective. Giving reassurance that you care and that you genuinely want to meet your spouse's needs can also make a difference. If your partner is very angry, you may have to be patient, since such gestures will probably be rejected at first—as a test of whether you mean what you say. Also, it sometimes takes a while for intense anger to fade. But if you are persistent in addressing your partner's hurt and sense of injustice, rather than the anger, you should be able to overcome it.

Another good way to address feelings of hurt and injustice is simply to apologize. This shows your partner that you care about his or her feelings enough to accept some responsibility for the problem. An apology costs little and can reduce anger faster than just about anything else you can do. There are many different kinds of apology, and some accept more responsibility than others, but *all* of them work!

For example, you can say: "I'm sorry"; "I'm sorry that you're angry at me"; "I apologize for interrupting you"; "I didn't mean that the way it sounded"; "I'm sorry if it seemed that I wasn't listening; I do want to hear what you have to say"; "I'm sorry that you've been so unhappy about our vacations over the last five years; I never understood that you felt so strongly about it."

Whether you apologize or offer some other caring gesture, responding to your partner's hurt and sense of injustice, rather than to the anger, will ease the hurt and allow you to return to constructive negotiation.

Return to the Negotiation Process

After summarizing how your partner feels, and addressing his or her sense of hurt, try to direct the conversation away from personal attacks and back to the problem. Refocusing on the negotiation process allows you to return to the rules of negotiation and avoids the pitfalls of the argument game. Say something like: "Let's get back to discussing your interests," or "Why don't we return to the brainstorming stage and see if we can come up with some more ideas." Problem solving what you will do in the future is much more productive than griping about the past, and it is the *only* effective way to resolve old relationship conflicts and to prevent new ones.

In summary, when your partner becomes angry and/or attacks you: listen quietly; ask questions to clarify; summarize how your partner is feeling and why; don't respond or defend yourself; address your partner's sense of injustice and hurt; then return to negotiating.

If you practice these techniques rigorously, you will find that emotions will cease to be an obstacle to negotiation, and real progress can be made in your relationship. Your job, then, is to avoid playing the argument game—even when you are attacked. If you refuse to play, your partner will have no one to argue with. Remember—it takes two to tangle!

13

Generalizing Your Negotiation Skills

In the previous chapters, the basic steps of negotiating and handling emotions were discussed. Of course, if every conflict had to be negotiated in such great detail, couples wouldn't have time left for anything else! Luckily, many issues can be handled by using a briefer version of the negotiation process. In this chapter, three forms of negotiation will be described: meta-negotiation, comprehensive negotiation, and brief negotiation. All three are based on the same principles, but each has its own use.

Meta-negotiation

This type of negotiation is used to resolve a conflict about the negotiation process itself. Meta-negotiation really means negotiating about how you are going to negotiate.

101

As noted earlier, the establishment of mutually acceptable rules for handling conflict can go a long way toward preventing it. To minimize conflict in business, most groups adopt well-established rules for conduct. In meetings, for example, sets of rules such as parliamentary procedure are used to dictate who can speak and when, to regulate the order in which issues are discussed, to provide an agreed-upon procedure for decision making, and to give authority to a chairperson to see that the group follows the rules and stays on track. The purpose of these rules is to keep the meeting focused on substantive issues and to avoid having the process itself become a source of conflict.

Similarly, when negotiating relationship conflicts, you need to follow rules that spell out how to proceed in the discussion. Adherence to these rules will prevent disputes over process. Indeed, when couples do get sidetracked into a fight about fighting, it is usually because they have deviated from the fixed procedure. Disputes about process seem to arise from three sources.

The first is when the process itself gets out of hand and spirals into a full-blown argument of its own. For example, if one person becomes slightly annoyed and raises his voice a little, the other may respond in kind. If each then continues increasing the volume, the partners may soon find themselves trying to outshout each other. In this case, there is no real issue. The process has merely gone out of control.

The second situation occurs when one or both partners have some concerns or fears about negotiating that haven't been aired. For example, they may avoid talking about sex because they are afraid that opening up this topic will reveal dissatisfactions.

The third situation occurs when one or both partners are angry or upset about another issue altogether, but instead of leveling with each other, they keep it hidden and express their discontent through other, safer issues, or by sabotaging progress in negotiations. These partners are bottling up an issue of real concern, and the anger and frustration associated with it are contaminating all of their other interactions.

Strategies to deal with each of these cases will now be discussed.

In the first case, where the process problem isn't based on anything very serious and is largely a result of partners not handling their emotions very skillfully, a "cease-fire" or time out can sometimes defuse the problem. Often the couple can return to negotiation after a time out without further ado. Alternatively, a brief meta-negotiation can be held to discuss concerns about runaway escalation and to reaffirm commitment to the negotiation. It may be a good idea to work out some precise rules for applying these techniques. For example, if shouting is the problem, you may wish to work out a specific plan to handle situations in which you begin to raise your voice.

In the second instance, the partners are concerned about the negotiation process and so get into a fight about fighting in order to avoid facing their fears. When Susan and Tom tried to have a negotiation session about who should help their daughter with her schoolwork, they quickly found themselves in the middle of a fight about fighting. Several minutes of bitter arguing ensued before they realized that they were no longer negotiating. After a twenty-four-hour time out, they held a meta-negotiation to redefine the ground rules for future sessions. One at a time, Susan and Tom discussed their needs, fears, and concerns about negotiating this issue, as shown below.

As they talked, it became clear that there were indeed some basic concerns about the negotiation process itself that had to be dealt with before they could return productively to the original issue. The meta-negotiation session disclosed that both Susan and Tom were fearful of each other's criticism, and these concerns were interfering with their ability to negotiate. By exploring their fears about negotiating, they were able to gain insight into each other's feelings and derive new ground rules, which made it possible for them to return to the original problem. Susan admitted that she was feeling a sense of personal failure. As a result, she had blamed Tom in order to keep him from blaming her. Tom reassured Susan that he did not feel that the situation was in any way her fault, and that, instead, he felt somewhat guilty for allowing himself to be so busy with work that he hadn't contributed. Meta-negotiation resulted in Tom and Susan agreeing that their negotiation on this topic should be strictly future-oriented rather than past-oriented. In addition, they agreed that they would do what they could to work out a plan for helping their daughter, and that they would try to avoid assuming or assigning responsibility or blame for their daughter's school performance.

Once they had shared their concerns and found a mutually satisfactory set of rules, both felt more comfortable about returning to negotiation of the original issue. Moreover, the act of sharing their fears about the process allowed them to identify the problem as "out there" rather than "between us." Having cleared the air of their personal concerns, they were able to give full attention to the original problem.

In meta-negotiation of this type, the conflict is about whether or not to negotiate, and each person discusses his or her fears and concerns about the negotiation process itself. Brainstorming involves thinking of ways to alleviate these fears so that negotiation can be used to tackle the original issue.

The third situation involves negotiating over the wrong issue. Typically, this occurs when one or both parties avoid the real issue because it is so sensitive that they fear it could lead to intense or uncontrollable conflict. Frustration and anger then spill over onto other areas and cause arguments

INTERESTS RELATED TO NEGOTIATING ABOUT DAUGHTER'S SCHOOL PERFORMANCE

Susan	Tom
• Concerned that Tom wouldn't listen	• Concerned about being criticized for not helping with homework in the past
• Concerned that Tom would accuse her of being overprotective if she expressed her concern over her daughter's school performance	• Concerned that he would be blamed
	• Wants to find a way to help their daughter
• Concerned that Tom would feel that she hadn't done a good enough job and hadn't been a "good" mother	
• Doesn't want to feel like a failure	
• Wants to share the problem	
• Wants to figure out how to help their daughter	

about anything and everything! However, because these conflicts are merely substitutes for the real thing, there is little genuine interest in resolving them. For example, when Susan and Tom sat down for their weekly session to discuss their finances, every attempt they made to negotiate turned into a fight about fighting. Although she hadn't said so, Susan was really furious with Tom for having (from her perspective) paid too little attention to her and too much attention to his secretary last night at the boss's party. Before they could proceed to any other issue, Susan's feelings of rejection and her fears about Tom and his secretary would have to be brought out into the open and discussed. If necessary, negotiation could then be scheduled to work out ways to avoid the recurrence of this problem in the future.

If you are getting nowhere in your negotiation, ask yourself and your partner whether there is some other, more important problem that needs to be dealt with first. These are sometimes referred to as "hidden agendas," and one or both parties can be involved in keeping an issue concealed. One party may have his or her own hidden agenda, of which the other party is only dimly aware; both parties may actively collude to avoid discussing a topic that is considered off-limits; or both parties may have their own quite different hidden agendas.

Often, hidden-agenda items involve core interests—such as the need to feel loved, concern about self-worth, fear of rejection, fear of failure, and so on. Talking about such basic needs can be difficult and may create strong emotional responses or blocking. Try to be sensitive to your partner's feelings and encourage him or her to get to the heart of these concerns, even if the process is painful. Don't challenge or belittle these concerns. Instead, try to be empathetic and reassuring. Often, just getting these fears out into the light of day and talking about them calmly and rationally can defuse them and clear the air. Fears such as Susan's may or may not be based on fact—either way, there is something important happening that should be discussed rather than ignored.

If you feel uncomfortable about going through this process on your own, you may want to consider getting professional help. Chapter 21 discusses what is involved in marital counseling and how to go about finding an appropriate referral.

Comprehensive Negotiation

The steps to be used in comprehensive negotiation were discussed in chapters 6 through 12. In comprehensive negotiation, each party explores his or her full range of interests and generates an exhaustive list of creative options as the basis for a win-win solution, as Susan and Tom did when negotiating plans for their vacation. A diagram showing the steps of comprehensive negotiation is provided on page 246 for later clarification.

Comprehensive negotiation is useful when conflict on the same topic occurs repeatedly. In these cases, partners may wish to have a negotiation not only over the particular instance that brought the issue to a head, but to negotiate more basic relationship rules to handle future occurrences of the problem. For example, to prevent future conflict, Susan and Tom may want to follow their negotiation session over this year's vacation plans with a session devoted to working out a set of basic rules for handling vacation planning in the future. The rules might involve scheduling of a regular, annual negotiation on this topic; rotating the responsibility for making vacation plans; establishing a formula for the number of exotic versus ordinary vacations; or adopting a rule about the number of days to be spent with relatives. Mutually agreed-upon relationship rules such as these can obviate the need for a yearly power struggle. You can deal with any problem that occurs repeatedly by establishing these kinds of relationship rules.

Disagreement about assigning responsibility for decision making is a commonly recurring source of conflict. Included in this are issues such as who decides where to live, when to move, the number of children to have, how much time to spend with the children, how to discipline the children, when to have social contacts, when to have sex, what to eat, and so on. Negotiating agreements about how to allocate decision-making responsibility can prevent later misunderstandings and recriminations. It is useful to remember that not all decisions need to be made jointly. The clear assignment of responsibility to one partner usually causes less conflict than vaguely shared allocations of responsibility. Richard Stuart, in his book *Helping Couples Change*, provides a useful breakdown of decision-making authority into five categories—those which are decided: (1) almost always by the wife; (2) by the wife, after consultation with the husband: (3) by both sharing in the decision equally; (4) by the husband, after consultation with the wife; (5) almost always by the husband.

One good way to review your rules is to make a list of all the areas in your relationship that require decision making. Then, working separately, each of you should go through the list twice. The first time, assign a rating of 1 to 5 (as specified above) to each area; rate how you think responsibility is allocated at the present time. When you go through the list the second time, note whether there are any areas where you are dissatisfied with the current allocation of responsibility and, if there are, record the rating that expresses how you would prefer it to be. When you compare notes with your partner, you will probably find some similarities and some differences in your ratings. Partners nearly always have different perceptions of how their decision-making responsibilities are divided. However, resist the urge to argue over whose perception is right. It's not relevant. What *is* relevant is the identification of the areas where one or both of you are unhappy with the way things are. These can then become the target of a comprehensive negotiation session.

When you sit down to negotiate this, write the contentious decision-making areas on the left side of a page, then record your respective interests to the right of each. Work your way down the list until you have a good understanding of both your own and your partner's interests. Now you are ready to begin brainstorming about how these might be allocated differently. One good rule of thumb is to assign the responsibility to the person who is most concerned about the issue. On the other hand, some issues may be best handled through joint allocation of responsibility, by simply taking turns or by brief negotiation each time the matter arises.

Once you have put your options together into a win-win solution, write down who is responsible for what, and keep the list where it can be taken out for review when necessary. Then, stick to your agreement! If you find that you are unhappy with some aspect of it, ask for a renegotiation session.

As previously mentioned, another major source of disputes is the allocation of responsibility for things such as household chores. Couples typically clash over two aspects of this: who will take responsibility, and how it will be done. One of the most frequent flash points occurs when one spouse doesn't approve of the way the other spouse does things. Responsibility can be real or illusory. *Real responsibility* is where one person agrees to do something and is allowed to do it his or her way on his or her schedule. *Pseudoresponsibility* is where one partner agrees to do something and the other tries to say how or when it should be done. Allocating responsibility, and then criticizing the person who has assumed it, is a sure way to make the sparks fly and to frustrate both partners. Therefore, it is important to decide who will be responsible and to further agree that the person who is allocated the responsibility will be given *real* responsibility to do it his or her way *without* interference, supervision, or reminding from the other. This simple rule can prevent a lot of conflict.

Usually, partners have different spheres of concern. As a general rule, it is best to allocate responsibility to the person who tends to be the most particular or the most concerned about the task. For example, if Tom feels embarrassed when the bank account is overdrawn and frets over paying the penalty, whereas Susan doesn't want to bother with balancing the checkbook, Tom should be given responsibility for that task. Susan can agree to record the amount of every check that she writes, or, if she doesn't want to do that, she can use cash instead. If Tom manages the account, Susan won't have to pay attention to it, but if Susan is given the responsibility, Tom will feel continually annoyed. On the other hand, Susan may be very fastidious about keeping the inside of the car clean. If she is assigned the job of vacuuming it regularly, Tom probably won't mind, but if Tom is given the job, Susan may feel let down. So, clear allocation of responsibility to the person who has the most concern about how a job should be done is the best approach. If for some reason the person who is less concerned does get the job, or if both are equally concerned, the best rule to apply is that the person who is given the job should be given *real* responsibility rather than pseudoresponsibility. The task may be traded back and forth, but during each person's tenure, it's up to that person to do it his or her own way—without criticism or reminding.

When negotiating rules related to responsibility, it is often useful to discuss all aspects of a problem at once, rather than tackle each separately. For example, a conflict over who does the dishes might lead to a fairer outcome if it is considered in the context of the whole range of chores. By putting everything on the table at once, you can be more creative in finding mutually satisfactory arrangements.

An example of Tom and Susan's negotiation over chores is shown on page 115. As shown there, Tom and Susan decided to include their son and daughter in the process, since parts of the negotiation directly involved them. To expand a negotiation session to include others, you merely go through the same process with more people. Explore each person's interests, include everybody in the brainstorming, and have them take part in building win-win solutions. Of course, children have to be old enough to understand the process in order to participate, but when they are, and when the negotiation directly involves them, it is a good idea to include them. In general, people (including children) are more willing to follow through on responsibilities that they have agreed to than on those that have been forced on them.

Notice that when Tom and Susan discussed vacation plans, they did not involve the children in the first round of their negotiation; instead, they held a separate session with the kids later, after they had resolved the conflict between the two of them. In cases where the children are involved but where relationship issues need to be dealt with first, you may wish to use this kind of two-stage process.

Tom and Susan also took this approach when working out what to do about their daughter's school performance. First, they held a negotiation session with each other to sort out the relationship issues related to their own concerns over criticism, personal failure, and neglect. After these were resolved, they sat down and brainstormed with their daughter. This allowed them to keep their daughter's problems separate from their own and increased the possibility of finding a satisfactory solution for everybody.

Of course, problems between couples that don't involve the children should be negotiated without them. Many families get into trouble because they try to negotiate several issues at once or because they include family members who shouldn't be involved. So, keep the negotiation limited to the parties directly concerned, or consider a two-stage negotiation when issues are complicated or when conflicts exist at several levels within the family.

While this book is focused primarily on conflict between partners, the negotiation method can be applied to any dispute and can also be used between a parent and a child or between two children (if they are old enough). Encouraging the whole family to resolve problems in this way is an excellent idea. It will make your family life more peaceful, and, through your example, you will teach your children skills that they will need to make their future relationships more satisfying. If you wish to read more about resolving family conflicts, consult *When Families Fight* by Jeff and Carol Rubin. (See the Further Reading section at the end of the book.)

Comprehensive negotiation takes time, but it is well worth the effort over the long run. Setting up relationship rules for how you will divide the chores may take five or six hours, but it can save you hundreds of hours of argument and acrimony. Reaching agreement on how to discipline the children may sound difficult, but it can save many a family row, create more consistency in your child management practices, and may even make you a better parent.

Brief Negotiation

Fortunately, not all conflicts require comprehensive negotiation. While many of the daily decisions that couples make involve some conflict, often they are not very important, and most of them can be handled by brief negotiation. This involves negotiating on the basis of interests, but instead of writing down each person's entire set of interests, each partner states only his or her primary interests. In place of brainstorming an exhaustive list of creative options, only a few are suggested until a solution satisfactory to both sides is found. Of course, if brief negotiation doesn't resolve the problem, a more comprehensive version should be scheduled.

Tom and Susan were home alone on Saturday night. Their daughter and son were at a friend's house.

TOM: I feel like being indulgent. How about if I make a cheese fondue?

SUSAN: I've been trying to lose weight and cheese is fattening. Can we think of something that is indulgent but not so fattening?

TOM: (Looking in the refrigerator) Well, we could have steaks and nice salad. There's a small steak in here with your name on it.

SUSAN: That sounds good. Would that satisfy your need for indulgence?

TOM: Yeah. I haven't had a nice steak for a while.

Notice that both Tom's need to be indulgent and Susan's desire to stick to her diet were satisfied with little difficulty. Of course, other win-win solutions were possible: for example, Tom could have had cheese fondue and Susan could have had steak. But another unexpressed need—to share a good dinner together without too much effort—probably was a factor in their decision to have the same thing. As shown, comprehensive negotiation was not necessary. Each person's most important interests were expressed and met by a brief search for a satisfactory accommodation. Additional examples of brief negotiation are provided in the following chapters.

Once you have established a mutually satisfactory set of basic rules that allows your relationship to function smoothly, brief negotiation can usually be used to resolve most of the less consequential day-to-day matters. Comprehensive negotiation can then be reserved for the more important or recurring issues.

The first half of this book has focused on learning negotiation skills. At this stage, some people assume that learning to negotiate means that they will have to give up arguing, and some express regret over this. However, learning how to negotiate does not mean that you can no longer argue, if you wish to. You certainly won't forget how! Instead, it means that you now have a choice. If you really want to argue, by all means do so. But it is a good idea to have a brief negotiation about it first, so that you both know what is happening. So, if you want to quarrel, explain your interests and decide together how you will proceed. Having a choice and knowing how to get out of an argument can give you the freedom to enjoy arguing, since you can now exercise some control over the process.

The next section explores some of the skills that can be used to prevent unnecessary conflict. They include thinking more constructively about your partner and your relationship, communicating more clearly, and getting rid of dirty tricks. Even more important is remembering to be affectionate, to have fun together, and to show that you care. The final section of the book focuses on the application of these skills to the most common sources of relationship conflict.

THE NEGOTIATED PLAN FOR HOUSEHOLD CHORES

Breakfast	Tom brings Susan coffee in bed by 7:00 Monday to Friday Susan makes breakfast Monday to Friday Kids make breakfast Saturday Tom makes breakfast Sunday
	Interests: • Tom needs to be at work earlier than Susan • Susan wants to sleep as late as possible • Kids want to sleep as late as possible • Tom and Susan want family to eat breakfast together
Lunch	Everyone eats at work/school during the week On weekends, whoever is inspired makes lunch
	Interests: • Everyone wants easiest arrangement • No one wants to fuss
Dinner	Susan makes dinner Monday and Tuesday Tom makes dinner Wednesday and Thursday The family goes out for dinner Friday Susan and Tom make dinner together on Saturday and Sunday
	Interests: • Tom needs to stay late on Mondays for staff meetings • Susan wants to attend evening meetings on Wednesday • Both are tired by evening and want some nights to relax

- Both are exhausted by the end of the week and want a break
- Both want to do some cooking together as a couple's activity

Washing	Susan takes responsibility most weeks; if she's too busy, the person who needs clean clothes the most does it
	Interests: • Susan worries about cleanliness
Ironing	Buy wash-and-wear clothes for the kids Susan and Tom do their own
	Interests: • Both want clothes ironed on own schedule • Both want to avoid arguments
Cleaning the kids' rooms	The kids are responsible for their own rooms Once a month Susan can clean the kids' rooms if she wants to
	Interests: • Everyone wants to avoid arguments • Susan worries about hygiene
Cleaning the rest of the house	The whole family takes part on Saturday morning Tasks are rotated weekly (the list of tasks will be negotiated next)
	Interests: • No one wants to spend much time on this • Everyone dislikes the tasks involved

Shopping for groceries	Susan and the kids do the bulk of the shopping
	Tom picks up things on the way home when necessary
	Interests: • Tom doesn't want to take the time
	• Susan wants to control her weight
	• Kids want to have a say in what is bought

Taking out garbage	Tom takes out the garbage
	Interests: • Susan is concerned about hurting her bad back
	• Tom likes the exercise

Balancing the bank account	Tom keeps the accounts balanced
	Interests: • Tom feels out of control if he doesn't know the bank balance
	• Tom feels embarrassed when the account is overdrawn
	• Susan doesn't want to worry about it

Paying the bills	Susan pays bills
	Interests: • Tom gets too worried about expenses
	• Susan wants to keep an eye on expenses so she knows when there is extra money and when there isn't

Taxes	Both go together to a tax consultant
	Interests: • Both want to avoid arguments that taxes have caused in the past
	• Both want to save time

Mowing the lawn	Tom does it when he has time When he doesn't, he hires the neighbor's son
	Interests: • Susan is concerned about her bad back • Tom likes to feel "macho" • Both feel that the kids are too young to handle it
Tending the flower gardens	Take care of them together as couple's activity
	Interests: • Both want to have fun together • Both like flowers
Filling the car with gas	Whoever is driving when it runs low
	Interests: • Neither wants to run out of gas
Having the car tuned	Tom takes care of this
	Interests: • Susan doesn't understand and "doesn't want to understand" mechanical things • Tom enjoys tinkering with the car
Cleaning the car	Susan keeps inside clean Tom keeps outside clean
	Interests: • Tom wants to project a good image to his clients • Susan wants to impress the neighbor who rides to college with her
Picking up and dropping off the kids at school	Kids get dropped off at school by Susan and picked up by Tom When both are busy, kids take the bus
	Interests: • Tom needs to be at work early

- Susan needs to be at college in the afternoon
- Kids didn't want to spend so much time on the bus

All of the above are subject to brief or comprehensive renegotiation as circumstances change.

III

Building
a
Lasting
Peace

14

Reexamining Your Thinking About Your Partner and Your Relationship

Psychologists have long known that how people think about things can affect how they feel about them. Thus, how partners think about each other and about their relationship can profoundly affect their feelings in this regard.

When couples fall into patterns of destructive conflict management, they often begin to dwell on the negative parts of the relationship and forget to think about the more positive aspects—even when they are not arguing. A large part of their self-talk may be silent criticism of the spouse. As they focus only on the negative, they develop a distorted view, which then begins to affect how they interpret events. If this goes on for long, partners may feel more and more pessimistic about the relationship and the possibility of changing it.

As mentioned earlier, couples in conflict frequently fall into a pattern of assuming the worst about each other's behavior. Instead of considering why the other person behaved in a certain way, or making a list of alternative theories to explain the partner's actions, there is a tendency to attribute any unsatisfactory actions to the other's undesirable personality traits. They tell themselves that the other person behaved that way because he or she is "insensitive," "unfair," or "selfish." This kind of thinking leads them to look for behaviors that confirm their ideas. They begin to interpret other behaviors as further evidence in support of their theories, and this convinces them that the partner *is* insensitive, unfair, or selfish. At the same time, positive gestures are discounted or attributed to circumstances rather than to genuine caring.

Sometimes people compare their less-than-perfect partner or relationship to an idealized partner or situation that they believe should or could exist, and they may then feel depressed, upset, or angry about not having things the way they imagine that they should or could be.

In other words, partners often perpetuate their own dissatisfaction and anger and create unnecessary conflict simply by the way they *interpret* their spouses' actions. Of course, if partners are able to resolve more of their conflicts, patterns of unproductive thinking will diminish. Tackling negative thinking at the same time as you are learning to negotiate is a good idea, since partners who are less angry tend to be more constructive negotiators. Learning to think more realistically can also increase positive feelings toward your spouse, and this in itself can help in reducing conflict.

Resist the Urge to Dwell on the Negatives

Many partners spend time reviewing their spouses' "faults." They ruminate over things the partner has done that angered them, and as a result they feel even more angry. Unfortunately, dwelling on the negatives just makes conflict more likely.

One of the simplest methods for controlling negative thinking is to replace it with positive thinking. Instead of dwelling on how terrible your partner is, think about some of his or her better qualities. Try to remember times when your partner was loving or caring. Initially this may be difficult, but it will be effective. Even a few positive thoughts can reduce discontent. As Tom drove to work, his mind was preoccupied with reviewing the argument that he and Susan had had over breakfast. As he remembered what she had said about his similarity to his mother, he became more and more incensed. In the middle of thinking about what he wished he had said, he remembered to think about something positive—the anniversary present she had bought for him and how she had driven all over town to find it. Then he remembered how great she had looked in it! This thought made him smile and took the edge off his anger.

Another approach to reducing critical thoughts is to try to accept some responsibility for the situation. Consider how you might be contributing to your partner's behavior. Have you been sensitive to your partner's needs? Are you making your partner feel unloved? Have you communicated your needs clearly and offered to negotiate? Have you told your partner that you want a win-win solution? Have you taken appropriate measures to alleviate your partner's feelings of hurt?

Recognizing that your behavior might be part of the problem can help you to feel less angry. It is also the first step in discovering what you can do to change your part of the interaction to make it more productive.

Refrain from Assuming the Worst

Many conflicts begin when couples assume the worst and interpret each other's behavior as intentionally critical or negative, when it was not intended that way. This can lead to conflict based on misunderstanding. When a couple is in constant conflict or under stress, there is often a tendency for both partners to react defensively to almost everything the other person does.

One way to combat assuming the worst is to consider some alternative theories to explain your partner's behavior. When Tom forgot to take out the garbage, Susan could have thought: "I wonder if he's doing it on purpose to annoy me," or, "He's been so worried about his mother lately, he must have forgotten." In both cases, Tom's behavior is the same, but how Susan interprets it will lead her to feel and act differently. In the first case, where Susan assumes the worst, she is likely to feel and act angry. In the second, she may be more sympathetic. Thus, it is Susan's *interpretation*, rather than Tom's behavior, that causes her to feel and act as she does.

People often attribute their feelings or behavior to a situation or event. For example, Susan may think that she is angry with Tom *because* he forgot to take out the garbage. But, again, it is how Susan interprets the event that makes her angry. In other words, Tom is not making Susan angry; Susan is making herself angry.

So, when we find ourselves assuming the worst, it can be helpful to question whether our interpretation is correct and to consider some alternative thoughts. When Tom arrives home to find Susan in a grumpy mood and assumes the worst, he might guess that Susan is angry with him. This can lead him to feel defensive and to stay out of her way. If, in turn, Susan assumes the worst about his response, she may conclude that he doesn't care that she's upset, and an argument will likely ensue. On the other hand, if Tom questions his first assumption and considers the alternatives—for example, that Susan might have had a bad day—this might lead him to behave differently. Instead of avoiding her, he might ask her why she is upset and listen sympathetically while she explains. Susan would then feel that Tom does care, and the evening would have a very different outcome.

An even more direct approach is simply to ask the other person for an explanation. For example, Tom could ask Susan to explain how she is feeling before he tries to mind read or to guess. However, it is important to ask in a way that doesn't sound like criticism, and to accept at face value what your spouse says. Partners sometimes doubt their spouses' answers and go ahead and assume the worst anyway, which gets them right back into the same fix.

If you are forced into a situation in which you can't ask and *must* interpret your partner's behavior, considering other reasons, rather than automatically assuming the worst, should help you to avoid unnecessary conflict. Give your partner the benefit of the doubt. "Innocent until proven guilty" is the principle of justice used by the courts, and it can be a good rule to adopt with your spouse.

Notice the Positives

Partners have a tendency to dismiss each other's positive gestures, attributing them to unusual circumstances or assuming that they were insincere. For example, Susan believed that she was being a loving wife when she stayed up until 2:00 A.M. typing Tom's submission to the board. But when Tom got up early to bring her coffee in bed, she believed that he did it only because he was worrying about the meeting and couldn't sleep. In this way, partners frequently discredit each other's caring gestures as something that the other didn't really mean. This kind of interpretation causes caring gestures to be devalued and brushed aside, rather than appreciated and cherished.

It is important, therefore, not to discredit these gestures. In fact, how you interpret your spouse's positive behaviors is just as important as how you interpret negative behaviors. If Susan surprises Tom with a nice meal after work, Tom can think: "She did it because she was trying to butter me up to get her own way about our vacation," or he can think, "She must really care about me." If he makes the first interpretation, even though Susan has worked all day making his favorite meal, he will feel resentful and manipulated. If he makes the second interpretation, he is likely to have a nice evening and to enjoy Susan's attention. Notice that in both cases, Susan's behavior is the same. Once again, the difference in Tom's feelings is due to *his* interpretations.

When your partner does something nice, why not believe that it is genuine? After all, you wouldn't want your partner to doubt the motivation of *your* caring gestures.

Modify Unrealistic Expectations About How Things Should Be

Expectations refer to the way people think things should be. Every person has expectations about how his or her spouse should and shouldn't be or what the spouse should or shouldn't do. Often, partners have not even thought through what these expectations mean or where they come from. For example, Susan had expectations that Tom should talk about his feelings, that family decisions should be shared equally, and that Tom shouldn't look at other women. Tom expected that Susan should take the responsibility for birth control, that she should stay home with the children when they became sick, and that she shouldn't wear sexy dresses to parties.

To complicate things even more, partners usually have expectations for themselves as well. For example, Susan agreed with Tom that she should stay home with the kids when they were sick. Further, she felt that she should agree to make love whenever Tom wanted to and that she shouldn't be the one to initiate sex. Tom believed that men should make the major family decisions, that he should be able to provide better, and that men shouldn't talk about their feelings, especially their insecurities.

As you can see, couples can have similar expectations, opposite expectations, and, in some cases, merely different expectations. When partners' expectations are similar, there is little problem, but when they are different, expectations can cause conflict. When we tell ourselves that things should or must be a certain way, it is not surprising that we become depressed, upset, or angry if they do not turn out our way.

Of course, one of the best ways to handle differing expectations is to use the negotiation process to find a satisfactory resolution. But before you do this, examine your expectations, consider where they came from, why they are so important, and whether they are worth keeping. Often, should-type expectations are formed during childhood. After all, our first learning about how families behave came from observing our parents, and there is a natural tendency to think that how our parents did it is how it should be. But this is not necessarily true, and these assumptions may need critical examination. Our parents lived in a different time, when cultural norms and expectations were different. Not only is the world a very different place today, but it is also possible that our parents' rules did not always make them happy, either.

As already discussed, expectations also come from what we are taught by our culture—through television, ads, magazines, movies, and so on. But these cultural stereotypes provide a very narrow (and not necessarily psychologically healthy) image of how "good" marriages should be and how "good" wives and "good" husbands should act. These rules are also worth questioning.

Determining what "shoulds" you are placing on yourself, your partner, and your relationship may require some thought. But once you have sorted them out, you are ready for the next step. If you find that your expectations are in conflict with those of your spouse, you may want to consider whether they are worth keeping. Sometimes it is best to abandon a belief that something should or must be a certain way and to accept things as they are. This is especially true when the source of unhappiness is merely one's interpretation that things are not right. By changing rigid beliefs about how things should be, partners can end up being more accepting and feeling happier.

Susan used to get angry at Tom because she thought that he should hang up his clothes as soon as he took them off, rather than throw them on the chair as he usually did. Tom believed that he should have the right to toss his clothes on the chair as long as he picked them up later. When Susan examined her expectation carefully, she saw that it originated with her mother, who was always worried that her aunt (who lived next door) would criticize her for not having a perfectly clean house. When Susan analyzed all the reasons why this expectation was no longer relevant or important, she decided that, indeed, it *didn't* really matter. Notice that by becoming more accepting, not only did Susan not take responsibility for hanging up Tom's clothes (that remained his job), but she gave up reminding or nagging him. The result was that both Susan and Tom felt better, even though the bedroom was a bit messier.

Of course, on some occasions you may decide that you want to retain an expectation of your or your partner's behavior. If your partner doesn't agree, you can always negotiate to reach a win-win solution.

Accepting That You May Not Always Win

If you are applying the negotiation model creatively, you should be able to arrive at win-win solutions for most of your differences in expectations. But what if you can't agree, or what if you do agree but your partner violates the agreement? Of course, you can always revert to your former tactics of anger or other punishing behaviors, but this is not recommended. Instead, you can express your disappointment and ask your partner for his or her suggestions about what to do. You can also let your partner know that this issue is really important to you and that you want to reach a mutually acceptable agreement. If you are still unable to reach agreement, set the matter aside for a while, then try to renegotiate at another time.

Another possibility is to accept that you can't always have things exactly the way you want them to be. This may seem strange advice, as the rest of this book encourages you to pursue your interests. But good negotiators always consider the entire picture and allow themselves a range of behavioral options. The well-known psychologist Albert Ellis has written extensively about how people make themselves unhappy with unrealistic and irrational beliefs that things should always be the way they want them to be. He suggests that learning to accept the things you cannot change is one way to be happier. This involves telling yourself that, although you would prefer that things were otherwise, you can handle it if they are not. Ellis notes that it is appropriate to be disappointed if something you want to happen doesn't happen, or if something you don't want to happen does happen. But he suggests that it is not useful to tell yourself that it is terrible and that you will be devastated. Further, he suggests that what people say to themselves about the situation will lead to how they feel about it and how accepting or unaccepting they are. If they tell themselves that "it will be terrible if I don't get what I want," they are likely to feel terrible. If they tell themselves that "although I will be disappointed, I can handle it," they are likely to feel more in control.

Although Susan had often asked Tom if he would give her a "hello" kiss, Tom still forgot whenever he was preoccupied. Susan used to think, "If he really loved me, he'd remember to kiss me." Susan's previous self-talk led her to feel hurt and depressed and sometimes it even ruined the entire evening. When Susan changed her self-talk to the following she felt better: "I'd like it if Tom remembered to kiss me hello, but if he doesn't, it doesn't really matter. I don't need a hello kiss to know that he loves me." This self-talk allowed her to dismiss Tom's behavior without getting overly upset.

Tom also tried this strategy. When Susan put on her sexy black dress for the party at his boss's house, Tom thought to himself, "I would prefer it if Susan didn't look so sexy because I feel a little jealous, but I can handle it. After all, she should have the freedom to wear what she wants, and these jealous feelings are *my* problem." Furthermore, if he had interpreted her behavior to mean that she wanted to look sexy for him, rather than assuming the worst—that she wanted to look sexy for the other men at the party—he might also have felt better.

Thus, examining your expectations of yourself, of your partner, and of the relationship can be important. Learning to be more accepting of your own and your partner's behavior is one way to avoid unnecessary conflict. Being more accepting of your partner's behavior does not, however, mean that you should accept bad treatment. Instead, it means that you are willing to examine your own expectations to make sure that you are not imposing unrealistic or unfair expectations on your partner. Most people have experienced changing their attitude to another person's behavior. The other person doesn't change, but you become more accepting. If you can do this, your partner will likely be more accepting of you, and you will both be better off.

Give Up Unrealistic Expectations About How Things Could Be

When partners are feeling frustrated with each other, it is common for them to think about an idealized partner or relationship and to compare their current relationship to this fantasy. Sometimes these fantasies are in the abstract; at other times someone real becomes the object of the fantasy: "If only I were married to her [or him], things would be different." Although it is useful to think about how you would like things to be, so that you can ask your partner for the things you want, it is not very useful to spend too much time in wishful thinking. It is unproductive because it is unrealistic. Fantasies about idealized relationships are just that: They don't exist. When two people live together, there are always problems. In fact, trying to work them out can be half the fun! If you *could* find an idealized relationship, you would probably be bored. Comparing your real partner to a fantasy one will only make you more depressed and dissatisfied and will interfere with attempts to make your current situation better. So, try to resist this temptation. Instead, consider what you can do to improve the relationship that you have.

Remember That Change Is Possible

Couples in conflict often get into the bad habit of pessimistic thinking about their relationship and their abilities to change it. Of course, the best antidote to this is change in the relationship, and learning to think more optimistically can help create change. Thus, whenever you catch yourself having pessimistic thoughts, try to replace them with more optimistic ones. Thinking pessimistically can lead to a "self-fulfilling prophecy," in which you actually convince yourself that things are hopeless. This thought can cause you to stop trying, and then of course change won't occur.

On the other hand, thinking optimistically will allow you to convince yourself that things can be changed, and this can affect how hard you work on the relationship. Hence, it is important to pay attention to your self-talk and to replace hopeless thoughts with more positive ones. When Susan thought, "I've tried and tried to change him and I can't! I'm fed up! What's the use in trying? He never listens. . . . I give up!" she felt so discouraged that she stopped trying to make things better. When she changed these negative thoughts to more optimistic ones, she felt more confident. Her new thinking went like this: "Tom and I haven't solved all our problems, but we're trying! If we can just keep practicing these skills, things will gradually get better. Building a good relationship takes time. I've got to be patient and do my part."

In summary, how you think about your relationship can affect how you feel about it and how you behave. It is easy to fall into bad habits, with pessimistic thoughts taking over and making things worse. Paying attention to what you are thinking and trying to replace negative thinking with more helpful, flexible, and optimistic evaluations of your partner and your relationship will make a big difference. So, resist the urge to dwell on the negatives, try to refrain from assuming the worst, don't allow yourself to generalize, notice the positives, modify your unrealistic expectations of how things should be; give up unrealistic expectations of how things could be; and remember that change *is* possible!

15

Turning Complaints About the Past into Requests for the Future

The importance of exploring our needs and concerns once a conflict has occurred has been discussed. Now we will see how expressing needs and concerns can also *prevent* conflict. Many people feel embarrassed about communicating their needs and sometimes even about having them. But communicating our needs to a partner is a basic human skill that is necessary to achieve understanding and intimacy and to avoid chronic frustration.

Expecting Your Partner to Read Your Mind

People in long-term relationships sometimes come to feel that their partners don't care about their needs. One of the major reasons for this misunderstanding is that the partner often doesn't know what the person's needs are—because he or she hasn't expressed them. Many of us have acquired the bad habit of expecting our partner to somehow magically know what we want and why. We seem to believe that because we've lived with this person for a long time, he or she should know what we want. It's almost as though we expect the partner to be able to read our mind, and, when he or she doesn't get it right, we think that this indicates insensitivity or lack of love, and therefore we feel hurt or angry. The following examples illustrate the problem:

(At the supermarket)
SUSAN: Do you want to buy some grapes?
TOM: No, not especially.
SUSAN: Okay.

(On the weekend)
SUSAN: What do you want to do today?
TOM: Anything.
SUSAN: Let's go to a movie.
TOM: I'm too tired.

In the first example, instead of stating her wishes clearly— "I'd like to buy some grapes"—Susan asks Tom what he wants. Had she stated her desire, it is likely that Tom would have happily agreed. But instead she expected Tom to mind read. Even after Tom had said that he wasn't interested, Susan could still have redeemed the situation by saying: "Well, I'd like some anyway." But instead she merely agreed and spent several minutes thinking of Tom as an "insensitive cad." What's more, she didn't get the grapes she wanted. Such episodes can add up and cause frustration and discontent.

In the second example, Tom had his own desires and *wasn't* willing to do "anything." But instead of telling Susan about them, he left her feeling set up and frustrated when he vetoed her suggestion.

Learning to express your wishes clearly is an important part of good communication. Since it is impossible for partners to meet each other's needs if they don't know what they are, learning to tell your partner what you want is the first step. Being assertive about your needs involves letting your partner know what you want, what you think, how you feel, and how you see a given situation. Being assertive allows both you and your partner to be open and honest and contributes to a deeper sense of sharing and intimacy. It also allows you to understand and to be understood, thus preventing conflict based on misunderstanding.

Some partners confuse assertion with aggression. But they are very different. Aggression involves trying to impose your wishes on another person. Assertion involves *expressing* your wishes, not imposing them. Aggressive behavior involves insisting on having your way and using dirty tricks or other coercive tactics to achieve it. Assertive behavior involves an honest statement of what you want.

Some people feel too inhibited to be appropriately assertive, fearing that expressing their wishes might appear selfish. As children we were taught that to be selfish is bad. In learning this lesson, many of us drew the wrong conclusion. The undesirable aspect of selfishness is not concern with one's interests, but the failure to consider the other person's interests. Pursuing your interests will enhance your relationship if you do it in tandem with concern for your partner's interests. Aggressive behavior is selfish. Assertive behavior is *not*. It is important to be committed to your personal growth, and this involves finding out who you are and what you want. Indeed, *not* letting your partner know what you want and how you think or feel may be selfish.

Another reason why some people are unassertive is fear that their desires might be in conflict with those of their partner and that their expression might create a quarrel. But not letting your partner know what you want is actually more likely to cause conflict, because it leads to a gradual build-up of frustration, which ultimately results in an aggressive outburst, usually triggered by some insignificant issue. Indeed, suppression of needs, followed by occasional bursts of aggressive frustration, is a common pattern for those who tend to be unassertive. Unfortunately, this pattern doesn't allow partners to learn the real source of each other's frustrations, so they have little opportunity to correct their behavior. Hence, they continue to behave in ways that disappoint each other's needs.

Making Simple Requests

Many problems can be overcome by learning to make simple requests, which is surprisingly easy. However, if you are not used to asking for what you want, you will need to practice. For one thing, needs are sometimes so repressed that you may not be aware of them until they are denied. For those who have trouble identifying needs before a crisis arises, the way to begin is to review situations in which needs have been frustrated. Then, pinpoint your needs in that situation and think through how you could have asked for them to be met. Next, try to identify similar situations *before* they occur and ask yourself, "What do I want?" and "Do I have any needs here?" Once you have identified your needs, all you have to do is say: "I want . . ." or "I'd like . . ." followed by your request. For example: "I want a hug"; "I'd like to make love"; "I want to discuss our finances"; "I'd like you to make dinner tonight"; "I want you to tell me when you're depressed." Notice that all these requests are *specific* rather than vague. "I want a hug" will get a better response than "I wish you were more affectionate," which sounds like criticism and doesn't communicate exactly what you want. Simple requests are also more effective when they are positive rather than negative. "I'd like you to make dinner tonight" is better than, "I wish you didn't always sit in front of the television set and leave dinner to me."

"I'd like you to make dinner tonight" is clear communication. It is hard for your partner not to understand what you want, and it is more effective than indirect communication, such as grumbling about sexism, hinting that you are tired, or raving about what a fantastic cook someone else's spouse is. Making a request will often result in willing compliance by your partner. Notice how much easier it is when Susan simply states what she wants:

SUSAN: I'd like to buy some grapes.
TOM: Fine.

SUSAN: I'd like you to make dinner tonight.
TOM: Sure. Any special requests?

Of course, your partner may or may not agree to comply with your request, but if not, you can have a brief negotiation so that you can have your needs met in another way.

SUSAN: I'd like you to make dinner tonight.
TOM: I'd rather not because I have so much work to do for the board meeting tomorrow. Why don't we go out for a quick meal instead?
SUSAN: Okay, or we could just order some pizzas to be delivered.
TOM: Good idea!

SUSAN: I'd like to go to a movie this weekend. How would you feel about seeing a film tonight?

TOM: I'm still exhausted from last week, so I'd prefer to stay home. But I'll be up for a movie by tomorrow night—or you could take the kids tonight without me.

SUSAN: I really wanted time with you. Let's have an early night tonight and see a movie tomorrow as you suggested.

TOM: Great!

In these examples, both Susan and Tom were clear about their interests, but at the same time they were also sensitive to each other's needs. As a result, it wasn't hard for them to arrive at mutually satisfying solutions with a brief negotiation.

Remember that practice makes perfect, and you may need to make a conscious and sustained effort to become skilled at communicating your needs. Some areas will be more difficult than others. Communicating simple requests about what you want during sex is often one of the most difficult. This will be discussed in chapter 19.

Learning to Say No

Learning how to say no to your partner's requests is just as important as asking for what you want, if you are properly to assert your own needs. Unassertive people often feel that they have to do whatever is asked of them, and they may even feel guilty when they don't. This is such a common response that one of the better-known books on assertion is titled *When I Say No, I Feel Guilty,* by M. J. Smith.

If your partner makes a request that conflicts with your needs, say so, as Tom did when Susan asked him to make dinner. Say honestly how you feel and why, then have a brief negotiation to see if you can find another way to meet both of your needs. This is far better than going along with a request that conflicts with your needs. If you forgo your interests, you will feel resentful and will be likely to take it out on your partner—in which case you both will lose. Ironically, if you say no, you both can win because you can then brainstorm creative ways to satisfy both partners' needs.

Requests, which are positional in nature, are only one possible solution to getting your needs met. If your partner has chosen a position that doesn't satisfy your interests, look behind the position to understand your partner's interests and see if the two of you can think of another way to meet them that doesn't conflict with your interests. In the following example, Tom makes a request of Susan that conflicts with her needs. Instead of abandoning her needs to meet Tom's request, Susan works with him to find a mutually satisfying plan.

TOM: Would you help me by typing my submission to the board on Monday night?

SUSAN: I'd like to, but I've got a meeting that night. I could do it on Sunday instead.

TOM: I won't have it written by then.

SUSAN: What about asking your secretary if she could do it for overtime pay? We could pay her ourselves if the company isn't willing.

TOM: Okay. And if she can't do it, maybe I could ask the person who replaced her when she was sick. She was an efficient typist.

Notice that Susan stands up for her interests without apology. Tom's acceptance that Susan's needs are important allows them to look for a win-win solution. Had Susan given in to Tom's request, she would have felt angry, and Tom would probably have felt guilty.

Of course, there may be times when you decide that your partner's needs are greater than yours and where you can't find another solution. In such cases, you may want to agree, as part of your win-win solution, to place your partner's needs temporarily over yours. However, as discussed earlier, reciprocity over time is important, so you will need to be sure that a balance is achieved, or you may want to negotiate an exchange as part of your agreement. If you determine both parties' interests and creatively brainstorming options, in most cases you will come up with a workable solution that will meet your partner's needs and will allow you to stick up for your own as well.

Indeed, if you can agree to ask each other for what you want and to say no to each other's requests in cases where your interests are in conflict, you will soon be communicating more honestly. In cases where your needs conflict, use negotiation to look for a different answer.

Cross-Complaining

Although partners are often reluctant to say what they want, they don't seem to have much trouble saying what they don't want. Complaining seems to come naturally to most couples. But complaining is not an effective way to bring about change, since it normally generates hurt and angry feelings and leads to defensiveness and "cross-complaining." This occurs when one partner's complaints lead to counter-complaining from the other. The following are examples:

SUSAN: You always leave the bathroom sink a mess.
TOM: You should talk! You leave your make-up all over the counter.

*   *   *

TOM: You're becoming as obsessive as your mother.

SUSAN: At least I'm not lazy, like yours!

*   *   *

SUSAN: You never kiss me anymore.

TOM: You always refuse my approaches.

SUSAN: That's because you don't approach me right.

TOM: How am I supposed to "approach you right" when you won't tell me what to do?

SUSAN: I've tried to, but you never understand!

TOM: You're always so reluctant to talk about sex that I don't dare ask. And when I do, all I get are vague answers.

Cross-complaining can go on for hours. Notice that most of these complaints begin with the word *you* and tend to blame the other person for something he or she has or has not done. This kind of criticism threatens your partner's self-esteem. No one likes to feel like a "bad" person, and the natural tendency is to reject the criticism by criticizing the partner in return, as shown above, or by becoming defensive, as shown below:

TOM: Why can't you remember to write down the amount of the check when you buy groceries?

SUSAN: You wouldn't remember either if you had to shop with two kids pestering you to buy everything in the store!

*   *   *

SUSAN: I'm sick and tired of you getting home so late!

TOM: I can't help it. You should see the stack of work I have at the moment.

Partners cross-complain or defend in an attempt to reject the criticism and preserve their self-esteem. However, rejecting each other's criticism means that complaints are not likely to be heard or behaviors changed. If your complaints are to be listened to, they will have to be put in a way that does not present a threat to your partner's self-esteem.

Making Requests for Change

The best way to do this is to use "I-statements." These begin with the word *I* instead of *you* and express how the speaker feels. They are less threatening because the speaker takes responsibility for the feelings involved. I-statements follow the formula:

- I feel . . . when you . . .
- In the future I'd like it if you would . . .

For example, Susan could have said: "I feel annoyed when you leave the bathroom sink dirty. I'd like it if you would clean up after you shave."

The statement conveys a specific feeling about a specific behavior and makes a specific request about future behavior. Although it is still possible for such statements to lead to cross-complaining or defensiveness, they are more likely to be heard, and your partner will have a clearer idea of how to avoid the problem in the future, since the complaint about past behavior has been turned into a specific request for the future. Remember—the past can't be changed, but the future can!

TOM: I feel nagged when you remind me to hang my clothes up. I'd like you to let me take responsibility for it myself.

SUSAN: I feel unloved when you don't kiss me good-night. I'd like it if we could cuddle when we go to bed— like we used to.

TOM: I feel rejected when you refuse my advances. I'd like to talk about how to interest you in sex again.

TOM: I feel frustrated when you forget to write down how much you spent on groceries. I know it must be hectic shopping with the kids, but can we figure out a way to get the total recorded?

SUSAN: I feel neglected when you come home so late. I'd prefer it if you would come home earlier.

Saying "I feel neglected when you come home so late" is much more likely to be listened and responded to than saying "I'm sick and tired of you getting home so late!"

Nonverbal behavior is also important when you are making requests for change. Look at your partner when you speak. Make the request calmly. Monitor your gestures and tone of voice to make sure that they are as calm and reasonable as possible.

If your partner still reacts defensively, try leaving out the "I feel" part of the statement and merely make the request for change: "I'd prefer it if you would come home earlier." If your request for change is ignored, acknowledge your partner's perspective and repeat the request. If that does not lead to results, suggest that you explore each other's interests and search for win-win solutions through either a brief or, if necessary, a comprehensive negotiation. Here's an example:

SUSAN: I'd like it if you came home earlier.

TOM: (Defensively) You don't understand how difficult it is to get away from the office.

SUSAN: I'd like to. Tell me about the problems, so I can. Then I'll explain why it's so important to me, and we can try to come up with some creative solutions. Okay?

TOM: (Still defensive) Okay. But I still don't see why it has to be such a big deal!

SUSAN: (Calmly) I'll explain why in a minute. First, tell me about the hassles of leaving work earlier so I can understand what the issues are for you.

TOM: Well, first, the boss stays late and I worry that he'll think I'm not pulling my weight. . . .

As can be seen, genuine interest in the other's perspective and concerns can disarm even the most defensive or complaining spouse.

In order for simple requests and requests for change to be effective, both of you must agree to use them. This will reduce tension in several ways. First, you'll have a better idea of your partner's needs and wants, and since it will be your partner's responsibility to tell you, you won't have to guess, nor can you be blamed for not guessing correctly. Second, you will be able to express your needs and wants more openly, rather than vainly hinting around and then feeling angry that your partner wasn't sensitive enough to take the hint. Moreover, since both of you are asking for what you want, neither will need to feel selfish when a request is made. "I statements" from one person in the relationship will promote "I statements" from the other. These can go a long way toward eliminating arguments based on mind reading. And, whether you agree to make the requested changes or to negotiate to find a different solution, you will be changing behavior in ways that eliminate the irritation that your past behavior was creating. Finally, don't be afraid to bring up trivial matters, because they are what most partnership conflicts are about. Resolving grievances when they first arise, instead of letting them become a repeated source of irritation, can dramatically reduce conflict.

Responding to Your Partner's Requests

Learning to be responsive to your partner's simple requests or requests for change is as important a skill as learning to make them yourself. When you listen, try not to become defensive. Use self-talk, if necessary. And be careful not to overgeneralize or exaggerate the meaning of your partner's request for change. The fact that your partner would prefer it if you did a better job cleaning the bathroom sink does not mean he or she thinks that you are a bad person—nor does it mean that your mate doesn't love you. Instead, it means that he or she wants the kind of honest relationship in which grievances can be aired, requests for change can be made, and changes in behavior can occur to minimize future frustrations.

Try also not to become defensive when you listen to your partner's requests for change. Listening does not necessarily mean that you will agree. Instead, it means that you acknowledge and are willing to respond—either through considered agreement or through negotiation. If you are able to meet your partner's simple requests or requests for change without compromising your needs, do so. This will build goodwill, which will make your partner more willing to reciprocate, and you will be taking your share of responsibility for making the frequent adjustments necessary to keep all relationships running smoothly. However, if your partner's request conflicts with your needs, use negotiation to find ways to meet your partner's interests without sacrificing your own. If a brief negotiation doesn't work, schedule a more comprehensive session.

Partners who are accustomed to confrontation may need more practice at making simple requests and requests for change in a manner that is not inflammatory. In such cases, it is important to adhere to the assertion formula and to make requests in a calm and rational voice and when you are not angry. Writing down your request is also an excellent idea.

You can revise it until you can get the wording just right, so that you can make the request in a way that is least likely to threaten your partner's self-esteem and *will* allow him or her to hear and respond without becoming defensive. A good way to test your approach is to imagine how you would feel if your partner made the same request of you.

Partners who tend to avoid conflict are even more likely to have problems making simple requests or requests for change and will need to practice this skill diligently. When such individuals do try to state their needs, they often express them in an indirect manner. The same recommendation applies in these cases—write out your request and present it at the beginning of the negotiation session. Also, remember to make your request as direct as possible, using wording similar to that shown in the examples above. Self-talk can be used to overcome your fears of conflict. If your partner becomes angry or defensive, suggest that you negotiate, and if the negotiation becomes an argument, suggest that you take a break to give your partner time to think it over. If after practicing you still find it difficult to make simple requests or requests for change, you may want to consider seeking some form of assertiveness training. (See the Further Reading section at the end of the book.) Also, many psychology clinics and psychologists in private practice offer such training, often in a group setting.

Encouraging Your Partner to Express His or Her Needs

In addition to stopping yourself from expecting your partner to read your mind, try to avoid engaging in the same kind of guesswork regarding your spouse. Don't assume that you know what your partner wants. You will probably be wrong, anyway. If he or she hasn't told you what you need to know, *ask* and then *listen*. If your partner is still reluctant, a little gentle probing, such as Tom did, may help:

TOM: I'd like to sleep late on Sunday morning. What do you think?

SUSAN: I don't care.

TOM: I feel frustrated when you don't express your opinion. I'd like to know what you want to do.

SUSAN: I guess I'd prefer to get up early so I can get the house cleaned before Mom comes. But you don't have to.

TOM: I had forgotten about your mother's visit. What if we worked on it together on Saturday? How would that be?

SUSAN: Okay.

TOM: Is there anything else you planned to do Sunday morning?

SUSAN: I was going to make some pies.

TOM: Could you make those Saturday while I work on the house?

SUSAN: Sure.

TOM: If we got the pies made and the house cleaned on Saturday, how would you feel about sleeping late on Sunday?

SUSAN: I'd like it. Then we'd be rested for Mom's visit.

TOM: Great. I really like it when you let me know what you want. It makes it so much easier for me to meet your needs.

SUSAN: Thanks for caring!

Many people do not feel entitled to have feelings or needs and may have to overcome some old learning. Although you should not take responsibility for your partner, asking what your partner wants and showing a genuine interest and willingness to respond can help him or her learn that the rules have changed and now it's okay, even good, not only to have wants and needs but to express them. Of course, this doesn't mean that you should automatically acquiesce when your partner does finally state what he or she wants. Rather, you should begin the negotiation process.

If your partner has trouble converting complaints into requests for change, you can help by asking the following: "What specifically do I do that you don't like?; "In what situations does it occur?"; "What would you prefer that I did instead?" If you go through these steps, you'll have a better idea of what the complaint is, and you can then choose to change or negotiate, rather than remain on the receiving end of continuous, ill-defined complaints.

Rewarding Your Partner for Change

If you express a simple request or a request for change and your partner tries to meet your interests, let him or her know that you appreciate the effort. Rewarding your partner for change is very important. Change is not easy for anyone, and there need to be some payoffs if the new behavior is to be maintained. Expressing your appreciation will go a long way toward encouraging your partner to please you and to meet your needs. So, let your partner know that you have noticed the change and are happy about it. Try not to take even small changes for granted.

Remember: Partners who engage in mind reading are asking for conflict. By learning to make clear, simple requests by replacing complaints with specific requests for change, partners can do a better job of satisfying each other's needs and overcome the many minor, mutual irritations that occur in all relationships.

Learning to say, "I want . . ." or "I'd like . . ." is the best way to communicate your needs. Turning accusations that begin with "you" into statements that begin with "I feel . . ." can work wonders, especially when these include a clear message about the behavior that is troubling you and a specific request for a change, such as, "In the future, I'd prefer if you would . . ." Don't forget to make requests *positive* and *specific* rather than negative and general.

It is vital that partners be responsive to each other's requests. Requests can be met either by compliance (when they are not in conflict with your needs) or negotiation (when they are). It isn't easy to ask constructively for what you need or for change. So, when your partner makes a request, don't ignore it. Being responsive to each other's needs will encourage clear and open communication and avoid the unnecessary conflict that comes from mind reading, cross-complaining, or keeping needs bottled up.

16

Putting an End
to Dirty Tricks

In their desperation to be listened to and to have their needs taken into account, partners sometimes act in ways that are provocative and coercive and that ensure escalation of conflict. Generally referred to as "dirty tricks," most of these behaviors are learned from years of watching parental disputes. Some partners have seen so much fighting of this kind that they consider it the norm. Although often they are aware of the destructive potential of these tactics, partners resort to them out of habit, desperation, or lack of skill—rather than from malicious intent.

Occasionally, dirty tricks can bring about a desired short-term result, but rarely do they lead to a lasting solution. More often than not, they also damage the relationship. Therefore, it is important to put an end to these destructive behaviors. This task is not an easy one, however, since dirty tricks tend to be used when partners are feeling most vulnerable and out of control.

One place to begin tackling dirty tricks is with a meta-negotiation session, in which you can agree to negotiate about how to negotiate. During meta-negotiation, you share your concerns about the way you have approached problems in the past, and establish some ground rules about how you will, and won't, tackle problems in the future. Start by identifying the destructive tactics you both have used, but be careful not to fall prey to the temptation to blame each other. Remember that people use such tactics due to faulty learning, not because they are "bad" people. During your discussion, you may need to pay particular attention to handling emotions. Your objective in this meta-negotiation is to make an agreement to work together to put an end to dirty tricks.

Even after you have reached an agreement, there may still be times when you inadvertently fall back into your old, well-ingrained patterns. But don't be discouraged—this is normal. Rome wasn't built in a day, and neither are good relationship skills. Just keep plugging away. As new habits become established, the old ones eventually fade away.

Some of the more common dirty tricks are listed below, with suggestions for abolishing them. This list is not all inclusive, and you may be able to identify others. If you do discover additional ones, consider how they could be replaced using the skills already discussed.

Leaving the Scene of an Argument

Walking out in the middle of an argument is a common ploy used by partners when they become angry. They may drive away or take a walk around the block. Milder versions include walking out of the room or turning on the television. Although such behavior is usually motivated by the same urge to withdraw that motivates time out, its effects can be very different, since there is no explanation of what the person is doing and no time is arranged to discuss the issue later. When a partner leaves the scene of an argument without calling a time out the other partner usually feels punished and angry.

Walking out can be constructively replaced with time out. This eliminates the destructive effects while still meeting the need to withdraw in order to regain control over emotions. If you feel the urge to leave, pause, then tell your partner, as calmly as you can, that you are too angry to discuss the issue productively and need some time out to walk around the block (or whatever). Negotiate a time to resume the discussion in the near future. Then, exit without a scene—no door slamming or tirades! Since both partners can call time out when needed, and since it doesn't mean the end of the discussion, most partners can accept this approach.

The Silent Treatment

This dirty trick is similar to walking out, but in this case the person cuts off communication by refusing to speak. If the partner reciprocates, it becomes a vicious, unproductive cycle. Partners often don't speak to each other for hours, and some can keep it up for days. Cutting off communication is a very common response to conflict. This occurs even on the international scene, when nations get into conflict and break diplomatic ties. But this tactic is useless if the goal is real problem solving, since problems can't be solved if you can't discuss them. Moreover, this behavior is often interpreted as punitive, and thus it generates further ill will. And the longer it goes on, the more provocative it becomes.

Learning to control your emotions *before* you get to this stage is vital. So, call for time out before your anger gets out of hand. If you have not already done so, schedule the issue for a proper negotiation session.

If you and/or your partner have begun using the silent treatment, call a halt to it immediately by identifying what is happening and then expressing your desire to find a mutually acceptable solution. The sooner you interrupt this game, the better. Saying something like, "The silent treatment isn't getting us anywhere. Let's schedule a negotiation session so that we can deal with this problem more creatively. Okay?" You may also want to express your desire to improve the atmosphere between you. Say something like, "I'd like to make up," or take your partner's hand or give him or her a hug to break the impasse. Be careful, however, not to do this in a paternalistic way. If your partner rejects your gesture, don't become discouraged or angry. Persist! Your partner will eventually begin to realize that he or she is acting unreasonably.

Grumbling about your partner in a less-than-audible voice and then refusing to repeat what you said is another variation of the silent treatment. If you are prone to do this, replace it with an assertive statement, as suggested earlier. It's much more honest and effective.

Acting Out

Sometimes partners are so angry or frustrated that they want to do something dramatic to show how strongly they feel and to relieve their tension. Hence, they "act out." One type of acting out is externally directed; the other type is internally directed. Externally directed acting out involves such things as putting your fist through a door or window, or smashing, throwing, or pounding something. Violence toward another person also falls into this category, but because of its more serious nature, it will be discussed separately in chapter 19.

Internally directed acting out involves harming yourself or threatening to do so—for example, pounding your head or threatening to kill or mutilate yourself. Of course, this type of acting out may also result in real harm to yourself.

Neither form of acting out achieves anything useful. It merely leaves you feeling that you behaved like a child and you may also be left with unnecessary damage to yourself or your property. Regular negotiation makes it unlikely that you will experience such extreme levels of desperation, but if you do feel tempted to employ such tactics, use calming self-talk and take the urge as a cue to call for time out. After you have calmed down, write down your interests, then present them clearly when you return to (or start) your negotiation. At such times, it is also useful to try to take your partner's perspective and to consider what his or her interests might be. If you can come up with some creative options on your own, all the better. But be careful not to become fixed on a solution, since it is likely that you will not have taken *all* of your partner's interests into consideration. Nonetheless, thinking the problem through more analytically will help to calm you down and is a much more constructive response than acting out.

If you continue to have trouble with this, you may want to seek professional assistance to learn some new anger management skills, as suggested in chapter 19.

Threats

Sometimes partners use threats in an attempt to make the other person behave in a certain way. This is usually done under the belief that there is no other way to get the other to recognize the urgency of the issue and the need for change.

The most common threat—sometimes stated explicitly, at other times only hinted at—is that of ending the relationship. Although occasionally sincere, usually the person issuing the threat doesn't really mean it. Instead, the real message is: "I feel that you aren't listening to me, and this is important! I want to be reassured that you will take my needs into consideration in arriving at a solution."

The trouble with making a threat, when you are trying to say something else, is that you aren't communicating clearly. You are unlikely to get what you really want, and your partner is likely to feel coerced and hurt. In some cases, your spouse may even begin to make plans based on your threat, and those plans can sometimes take on a momentum of their own. So, instead of making a threat, try saying: "I'm worried that you will make a decision without taking my point of view into consideration. I'd like to be reassured that you *will* listen to my interests and that you *do* want to find a win-win solution to our problem."

Kitchen-sinking and Gunnysacking

These terms have been used to identify the ways in which partners expand their list of grievances. Kitchen-sinking refers to tossing everything into the argument except the kitchen sink. Gunnysacking involves bringing up old issues that have been accumulating in a "gunnysack."

If you make a point of scheduling regular negotiation, and if you bring up issues for special negotiation as they occur, you should be able to avoid both of these pitfalls. However, if they continue to be a problem, you may need to schedule negotiation sessions more frequently.

When, despite your best efforts, other issues creep in, ask if your partner wishes to negotiate these topics separately. If he or she agrees, set them aside to be dealt with at a later time, and write them on an agenda. Then, state your wish to stay with the issue you are already discussing. Do not let yourself become sidetracked by new issues until the one you are working on is resolved.

Dumping

To dump means to allow grievances from one situation to spill over onto another. Sometimes partners dump their frustrations, anxieties, and irritations on their spouse. When they are angry at someone at work, they take it out at home. Clearly, these partners are targeting the wrong person. Dumping is sometimes obvious but at other times it can be hard to detect. For example, the wife who is blamed when her husband hits his thumb with a hammer has a pretty good idea of what is really happening. But when the source of the frustration occurs outside of the spouse's presence, dumping can be more difficult to recognize.

In either case, dumping is unjust. If you are a victim of this tactic, you may want to name the game and suggest that your partner tell you about his or her troubles instead: "I feel that you are grouchy tonight for reasons that don't have much to do with me. Is something else wrong? I'd like to hear what is upsetting you." Often, having the chance to complain and be listened to will help to dissipate the bad feelings.

Partners who find that they have a tendency to dump may need to monitor themselves by asking questions such as, "Do I have a real grievance here or a real issue to negotiate, or am I just dumping?" Learning to be assertive about one's own needs and to negotiate win-win solutions to the *real* sources of frustration is, of course, the best way to put an end to dumping. You may need to apply to your work situation the negotiation and assertion principles explained in this book. In addition, other books on this topic, as well as assertiveness training, can be helpful.

Put-downs

Many actions that occur during runaway escalation make partners feel that they are being treated like a child. These behaviors are often so infuriating that they send the person into orbit! Such behaviors include finger pointing and finger shaking, making faces, sticking out one's tongue, hateful looks, saying "you never" or "you always," telling the other to "shut up!" and shouting. Name-calling and character assassination, which also fall into this category, will be discussed separately in the next section.

Some of these tactics make the recipient feel that he or she is being scolded like a naughty child (for example, when a partner shakes his finger disapprovingly). Others make the perpetrator seem like an angry two-year-old (for example, when one partner sticks out his or her tongue at the other). Although most adults don't appreciate being treated like children, they often react by responding in kind. Most of us experienced these kinds of put-downs when we were growing up, but it is certainly not appropriate to treat your spouse (or your children) this way. Put-downs escalate conflict, they don't solve anything, and they undermine positive feelings between partners.

When the urge to use a put-down arises, try to replace it with the more adult response of saying how you feel and why: "I feel ignored when you cut me off in the middle of a sentence." When your partner directs a put-down at you, a similar statement of feelings is much better than responding in kind: "When you shake your finger at me like you're the par-

ent and I'm the child, I feel offended. Please just tell me
what's upsetting you."

Character Assassination

Many intimate partners call each other names that they
would never even think of calling a stranger. Some spouses
use nasty names when they are angry; others use them as a
joke. Some only use them in private; others use them in public. Such names usually refer to some personal characteristic
that the person may or may not possess. Favorite targets are
intelligence ("stupid"; "dummy"; "idiot"), physical attributes
("ugly"; "fat-so"; "Miss Piggy"), or personality traits ("know-
it-all"; "wise-ass"; "jerk"). Some couples are quite creative in
this area: One husband who had an interest in Native American culture referred to his wife as "she who makes canoe sit
low in water." But even when used in jest, such put-downs
usually make the partner feel insulted and belittled. When
used in public, they can be humiliating.

The best way to stop these forms of character assassination
is to bring up the topic for meta-negotiation and agree to end
this behavior. It is easier if both partners try to drop name calling and insults out of their conversations at the same time, but
if only one partner takes the initiative, it is likely that the other
will eventually follow suit.

Try to give up this habit in all situations—even when you
are angry. If your partner calls you a name or insults you,
don't reciprocate! Instead, use a feeling statement: "I feel hurt
when you call me 'stupid.' "

When name calling and insults occur, it usually indicates
that you have not been sufficiently assertive about your needs
or that you have forgotten to use your negotiation skills. If
you had remembered, it is unlikely that you would be feeling

so irritated. So, the urge to use this dirty trick can serve as a reminder to apply your negotiation and anger-management skills. However, if you do slip up and call your spouse a nasty name or make an insulting remark, apologize. It will defuse the situation and help you remember not to do it in the future. Say something like: "I'm sorry I called you 'stupid.' I didn't mean it, and I'll try not to do that again."

Tears

Crying during an argument is a common occurrence, and usually it is the woman who cries. For many women, this is a natural response to feeling hurt, and when the hurts accumulate, as they do when conflict escalates out of control, many women cry to relieve the tension. Unfortunately, this is often misinterpreted by men, who tend to view crying as manipulative. This culturally trained difference between the sexes is the source of many misunderstandings. Simply accepting that, in general, tears mean that your partner is suffering will help put crying in its proper perspective.

In any case, when negotiation skills are used correctly, there is little need for tears, since the anger and hurt that cause them do not occur. So, if your arguments frequently end up in tears, brush up on your negotiation skills and stick to the formal rules of negotiation. Using calming self-talk, taking time out, and getting rid of the hurtful tactics discussed in this chapter should help.

If you do find yourself in tears, use them as a signal that time out is needed, and reschedule the negotiation. If it is your partner who is crying, try to give some comfort. Chances are you too will want a hug, and you'll get one a lot faster if you initiate it.

Even if you suspect that your partner's tears are a dirty trick, it is still best to put off further discussion of the issue until you can adhere to the rules of negotiation without interference from emotions. When you return to the negotiation, pursue your interests just as vigorously, but be certain to listen to your partner's interests as well. If you are faithful in following the negotiation method, it's virtually impossible for tears to be used against you.

Filibusterers

Partners who filibuster don't listen; they just talk. They try to hold the floor by whatever means possible and overwhelm the other person with a torrent of words. They not only talk nonstop, they scold the other person when he or she tries to interrupt. When the other person tries to talk about his or her interests, they act disinterested or assume that they already know what the other is going to say. They don't ask questions, they interrupt, they don't reflect or validate, and they "yes-but."

Partners who filibuster usually do so because they are afraid to hear what the other person has to say. They may fear that the other's message will threaten their self-esteem or be rejecting. Sometimes they fear conflict. Often they have an underlying insecurity about the relationship, and they fear that honest discussion will open a Pandora's box that can't be closed. Filibusterers also fear that the other person won't listen to what they have to say unless they are insistent. But often filibustering creates the very behavior it seeks to prevent. It causes the other person to turn off and to interrupt. Thus, the filibusterer ends up feeling that his or her point of view hasn't been heard and so continues to feel the need to get his or her message across.

Fortunately, there are a number of ways to handle filibustering. One is to let your partner have a say and to pay careful attention through active listening, reflection, validation, and summarizing, until there is nothing more to say and he or she has "run out of steam." When this is followed by reassurance that you will take your partner's perspective into account in finding a solution, usually the filibusterer's anxiety will be calmed enough to allow him or her to listen to you. Another strategy is to set time limits within which each side can discuss its interests. Asking each party to summarize and resummarize the other's interests can also *require* a filibusterer to listen.

If you are a filibusterer, you may want to carefully analyze your feelings and combat your fears with self-talk. Ask your partner to summarize your interests and to write them down until you are confident that you have been understood. Then, leave it at that. Don't explain all over again. Next, practice your active listening skills, and don't assume that you know what your partner is going to say. Give your partner your full attention, and don't interrupt except to ask clarifying questions. Don't try to refute your partner's point of view or restate yours when your partner is speaking. Reflect what you hear your partner saying and communicate that this point of view makes sense to you (even if you don't agree with it). Summarize what your partner has said. If you didn't get it right, ask more questions, listen carefully, and resummarize until you get it right. Finally, congratulate yourself on overcoming your tendency to filibuster and having had an honest communication with your partner without any disastrous results.

Unholy Alliances

Telling others—the kids, your mother, the neighbor, or your best friend—about your relationship problems for the purpose of getting advice or gaining allies is *not* a good idea. Third parties should not be brought into conflicts unless they are directly involved or you are seeking professional help.

You are the one who has to become proficient at asserting your needs and negotiating satisfactory solutions. No one else can do it for you. Moreover, involving others confuses the issue since they usually have their own agenda or interests, which are not necessarily the same as yours. Finally, your partner may resent that you have shared private information.

If your partner tries to bring others into your conflicts, let him or her know how you feel by requesting a change. Tom told Susan: "I feel really betrayed when you tell your mother about our problems and she tries to interfere. In the future, please don't talk to her about our personal problems." You can be equally clear and assertive with well-meaning or not-so-well-meaning relatives or friends, as Tom was when he responded to interference from Susan's mother: "I feel unhappy when Susan goes to you with our problems. I'd rather she talk to me directly. I'll discuss it with her, but not with you, since it's a personal issue between us that we have to sort out ourselves." If you clearly state how you feel and don't allow others to interfere, most people will give up. If you feel that you can't resolve your problems without advice from others, seek *professional* help. It will be much more reliable and won't further complicate the situation, as interference from nonprofessionals tends to do.

Martyrdom

People who don't stick up for their own interests and instead concede to their spouses' interests are not doing anyone a favor. Over time, this pattern causes a ballooning gunnysack of complaints and grievances as the partner increasingly forgets even to consult the compliant spouse about their needs.

Moreover, people who regularly allow their partners to win at their own expense often engage in a series of passive-aggressive tactics to try to readjust the imbalance. One of these is pouting. Pouting occurs when feelings of loss give rise to an urge to "get even," thereby letting the partner know that there *are* consequences. The partner who has won is subjected to a bout of moodiness as repayment for being insensitive. In fact, the person who resorts to pouting is often genuinely depressed about having his or her needs ignored, but doesn't know how to pursue them openly. Unfortunately, pouting rarely solves the problem, and, as the person who ends up in the martyr role suffers, so does everyone else in the family—including the children. In the process of trying to avoid conflict, the couple has created a prolonged conflict that simmers just below the surface.

Learning how to be more assertive is much more effective than pouting or other passive-aggressive tactics. Chapter 16 suggested that people who don't know how to ask for what they want can learn to do so. If you tend to give in, you may want to work on this systematically. If you still find it difficult, consider taking assertiveness training, or read some of the books on assertion listed in the Further Reading section.

The Unspoken Bargain

A related game is the "unspoken bargain." Here, one partner concedes on one issue in exchange for winning on another, but this is done without any negotiation, and the spouse is never told of the unspoken expectations. For example, Susan agrees to go to the football game with Tom, hoping that by doing so, Tom will agree to attend the PTA meeting with her. But Susan never negotiates this exchange, and when Tom turns out to have an appointment on the night of the PTA meeting, Susan feels betrayed.

The best way to overcome the unspoken bargain is to make all negotiations explicit. When Tom asks Susan to come along to the football game, she should mention that she'd like Tom to attend the PTA meeting and suggest that perhaps they could swap requests. Of course, Tom will still have an appointment, but if both of their requests are out on the table, they will be aware of the full situation and can then negotiate a solution that won't leave Susan feeling let down and Tom feeling set up.

The Psychoanalyst

One of the more sophisticated, but equally dirty, tricks is trying to psychoanalyze your partner's behavior. This is really just another attempt at mind reading and is usually employed by people who feel that their partner isn't being straight with them, but who don't know any way to find out what is really going on in the other person's mind, other than guessing. Because society teaches men not to be in touch with their feelings, while encouraging women to be very aware of them, it is more often women who feel this frustration. The difference is so pronounced that some men, when confronted about their failure to communicate, can't even understand the complaint.

Amateur psychoanalysts often realize that their unwanted interpretations will be provocative, but they engage in them anyway, in the desperate hope of gleaning *some* information about how their partner feels during the course of an argument. Partners who resort to this tactic often do so because they feel deprived of true sharing and intimacy. People in this bind need to encourage their partners to talk and to replace their analysis with active listening, which is, after all, what professional analysts do best. Patience is an especially useful attribute, because teaching a partner to explore the depths may take considerable time and careful nurturing.

Regular negotiation will also help this process. First, it will encourage both of you to explore the deeper issues behind your positions, and practice in this area can, in itself, help to increase communication skills. Second, it will provide a safe environment for discussing needs, wants, fears, and concerns, since the ground rules of negotiation provide reassurance and protection. Finally, the issue of intimacy can be scheduled as a topic for negotiation and you can both explore creative ways to increase it. All of these suggestions will work better than guessing. So, pursue your needs for intimacy, but consider more creative and effective ways of having them met.

Refusal to Negotiate

Partners sometimes take a firm positional stand and flatly refuse to negotiate. This tactic is particularly frustrating and can quickly wear away goodwill. Partners who refuse to negotiate usually do so because they feel uncertain about their negotiation skills and don't really believe that win-win solutions are possible. They fear that by agreeing to negotiate, they are likely to lose.

If your partner refuses to negotiate, try to initiate a meta-negotiation on the problem. Indeed, your wish to negotiate and your partner's wish not to is a conflict that can be treated just like any other. This kind of meta-negotiation can allow you to discuss your partner's interests in not negotiating as well as your interests in negotiating, and may result in some mutually agreeable rules that can be used to resolve the original problem.

Refusal to negotiate may also be caused by fear that the negotiation will turn into an argument. If your partner is fearful of face-to-face contact (fearing that it will become face-to-face combat), one means of opening the way to negotiation is to suggest communication through letters. Ask your partner to write to you, listing and explaining his or her own interests in regard to the disputed issue. You can then respond with a letter that begins with an acknowledgment and summary of your partner's interests, followed by an explanation of your interests. Creative ideas based on both sets of interests can then be offered. Invite your partner to add to the list in a return letter. Finally, try combining some of the options into win-win solutions, based on you and your partner's interests. Once again, you can invite your partner to reciprocate and then work on improving each other's suggestions until you find one that is agreeable to both of you. In other words, the whole negotiation process can be carried out by letter. This makes it easier to handle emotions and can be a good way to show your partner that problems *can* be solved without argument. After a few of your problems have been solved in this way, your partner may be more willing to try the method face to face.

Some of the more common tactics that contribute to conflict escalation have been discussed above. Identifying dirty tricks as they arise can be useful for both you and your partner, if you can do it in a calm, nonblaming manner. When you are on the receiving end, remember that the key is to resist the urge to respond in kind. Further, understanding that people resort to dirty tricks in desperation, when they have genuine needs that aren't being met, will help you to put them in perspective. Then, two options are possible to improve the situation. First, new, more effective skills can be learned to replace dirty tricks; second, you can become more sensitive to each other's expression of needs, so that dirty tricks aren't necessary. In fact, simultaneous use of both strategies is probably the best approach. Becoming aware of the urge to use a dirty trick, catching it before it occurs, and converting it into more constructive behavior will take considerable patience, practice, and maturity. But change *is* possible.

17

Making Love, Not War

One important source of conflict is neglect. All relationships need to be nurtured, but in the hustle and bustle of everyday life, many couples forget this. They lose sight of the importance of having fun together, being warm and caring, and inspiring each other to passion. Instead, they become so focused on their problems that they stop creating positive times together and expressing positive feelings. As the positive side of the relationship is neglected, each partner feels increasingly unsupported, unloved, hurt, and angry. Conflict is likely to be the result.

Relationships can be compared to an old-fashioned pair of scales with the negatives (for example, arguments) on one side, and the positives (for example, nice times together) on the other. If you concentrate too much attention on the negative side, the balance will be tipped in that direction. But if enough weight can be placed on the positive side, the scale will be tipped back. Or, consider a bank account: To keep a healthy balance, the (positive) deposits have to exceed the (negative) withdrawals. Research on marital satisfaction strongly supports the validity of these metaphors. Dissatisfied couples have more negative and fewer positive exchanges than satisfied couples do.

When partners show more thoughtfulness and respect for each other, conflict is diminished. The positive feelings that are generated by this behavior lead to a lowering of the threshold for "assuming the worst" and so partners are more likely to give each other the benefit of the doubt. Of course, unresolved problems will remain unresolved if they aren't tackled through negotiation. But even in the absence of negotiation, paying more attention to each other will likely make things better. In many cases, improving the quality of the relationship paves the way for major conflicts to be resolved and for change to take place. Partners are more likely to work harder on the relationship if they are feeling more positive about it and about each other.

Taking Your Partner for Granted

When couples begin romantic relationships, much of their initial behavior involves positive exchanges. Both parties try to look as attractive as possible and to be charming and likable. Positive gestures, affection, and gifts are common. Time together is spent having fun. When the "chemistry" is right, the net effect of all this is the feeling of mutual attraction that we call love. But as the relationship becomes more permanent, the pressures from work and/or children take over, many of these behaviors occur less frequently or stop altogether. Partners no longer devote as much time to their appearance. Affectionate behavior and romantic gestures become less frequent. Lovemaking occurs less often. The partners begin to spend more time worrying about problems, complaining, and arguing. As stresses on the relationship increase and the positive interactions diminish, the scales are tipped in favor of the negative side. The bank balance becomes overdrawn, making credit scarce and positive deposits by either party less likely. Not surprisingly, neglect of the relationship may cause partners to begin questioning whether they are, or ever were, "in love."

Falling in Love Again

The state of being "in love" receives a great deal of attention in popular culture and is the subject of countless songs, poems, novels, television programs, films, and magazine articles. Regrettably, most of these focus only on the first stages of romance, where partners are supposed to lose their heads, hear bells ring, feel all dizzy inside and think that the beloved is perfect in every way. This concentration on the early stage causes confusion for some people, who mistakenly believe that being in love means living in a chronic state of emotional fervor. They go from partner to partner looking for the intense emotion that they mistakenly identify as love, hoping that when they find it, it will last. And when their heart no longer goes "thump" in the presence of a particular partner, they assume that they are no longer in love, and go off on yet another, futile search. Sadly, some people spend a lifetime searching for the wrong thing.

No one can permanently experience the intense emotions that sometimes characterize new relationships. In fact, it would probably be unpleasant if one could. Rather, as love deepens, the butterflies in the stomach and the highs and lows of ecstasy and despair are gradually replaced by a deeper and more lasting sense of intimacy, acceptance, and respect for each other. This more advanced stage of loving is based on mutual affection and a sense of understanding that results from sharing intimate thoughts and feelings, hopes and fears, and learning to give and receive pleasure. It also encompasses a more realistic awareness and tolerance of, and empathy for, each other's imperfections.

Many couples can benefit from an awareness of these different developmental stages of love. Realizing that although their hearts no longer go "pitter-pat," they may still be in love (in an even better and deeper sense than they were in the early days) can be reassuring.

Of course, love can and does fade if partners neglect each other, or if they take their relationship for granted. People don't just fall in love and automatically stay that way. Love needs to be cultivated and cared for. Many couples report that they go through periods of being more, and less, in love. Not surprisingly, these periods almost always correspond to how much attention the partners are giving to each other and to their relationship. More often than not, this is related to how busy the partners have become with other things.

Fortunately, even relationships that have fallen into a state of serious neglect can be repaired if couples reintroduce the same kinds of affectionate behaviors that caused them to fall in love in the first place. Of course, because people change, these behaviors may not be identical to those they used during their courtship, but the principles are the same. Reintroducing loving and romantic behaviors into your relationship can be fun and can dramatically reverse the destructive effects of a gradual drift toward neglect of the relationship.

Initiating Positive Gestures

To reintroduce romantic and loving behaviors, some changes must be made. In keeping with previous discussion in this book, the most effective place to start is with changes in *your* behavior. Many people mistakenly believe that they have to *feel* loving before they can *be* loving. It is true that feeling affectionate makes it easier, but it is equally true that acting in an affectionate manner will make you feel more affectionate. Showing your partner that you care can reawaken positive feelings within you that have been suppressed by conflict and neglect.

What is more, change in you is likely to lead to change in your partner. Unilateral changes create a shift in the nature of your interactions. But to be successful you will need to maintain your own efforts for a period of time *regardless of your partner's initial response*. To change the pattern of a relationship that has been dominated by conflict requires perseverance. Partners may not respond immediately because they doubt your sincerity. However, if you continue your positive gestures regardless of the response, your partner will begin to see that you really are trying to make things better, and, once convinced, he or she will respond in kind. Relationship norms create a kind of reciprocity rule that makes it virtually impossible to remain angry or grouchy when the other person is bombarding you with loving behavior. Eventually the person being bombarded must give in and reciprocate or feel like a heel. Although it may take a while, if you persist, you are likely to break through the wall of anger and suspicion and find the real person on the other side!

There are many ways to be loving and romantic. Don't worry—you haven't forgotten them all! But in case you are out of practice, here are a few suggestions. One way is to have more fun together. Another is to increase the amount of physical and verbal affection between you. Gifts, loving gestures, and romantic surprises are all effective. And, of course, having more and better sex can help. If you are willing to accept some responsibility and take the initiative, you can introduce all of these back into your relationship with surprisingly positive results.

Reintroducing Fun

Research has shown that couples who share more enjoyable activities, called "coupling activities," get along better. So, if you have forgotten how to have fun as a couple, sit down together and consider what coupling activities you might enjoy. You may want to consider things you used to do as well as new ideas. The keys to developing coupling activities are creativity, imagination, and willingness to try an activity even if you're not sure that you will enjoy it.

Coupling activities can involve going out together—for example, movies, plays, concerts, dance, live entertainment, sports events, exhibits, art galleries, or anywhere else you can think of. Or they can involve learning to do something new, such as sailing, skiing, painting, playing bridge, making pottery, dancing, playing golf, or developing your own photographs. Coupling activities might also include something you've enjoyed in the past, such as camping, fishing, gardening, backpacking, boating, making your own Christmas cards, and so on. You may want to take up a joint hobby, such as buying antiques, birdwatching, stamp collecting, etc. Or you may prefer simple activities that you can do together, such as reading a book, doing crossword puzzles, playing chess, reading the paper, giving each other a massage, listening to music, sharing a bath, jogging, watching the sunset, or taking a walk. Food can offer additional opportunities for good times: you can go on picnics, try new restaurants, sign up for a cooking class, start a wine cellar, have a luncheon date, or cook a nice meal for friends.

Vacations and weekend getaways are another important source of coupling activities. Couples are sometimes reluctant to leave their children behind, but couples need time alone if intimacy is to be regained and maintained. Of course, the freedom to do this depends on many circumstances. But even going to a motel for a night or a weekend can do wonders. Getting away for a week or two every now and then can be even more rejuvenating.

One of the favorite excuses for not doing coupling activities is: "We haven't got the money." Indeed, some of the above examples do require more income than many couples have. When money is a problem, finding coupling behaviors merely requires you to be a bit more creative. If you give it enough thought, you will discover that there are literally hundreds of enjoyable things you can do together at little or no cost. Playing in the snow, reading to each other in bed, baking bread, learning to identify the constellations, browsing in stores, looking at old photographs, reading the Sunday paper aloud, going to the library, riding bikes in the country, taking a shower together, and listening to records aren't very expensive but can be lots of fun.

Another common excuse is: "We don't have enough time." Time problems can usually be remedied with a little planning. Look for other activities that can be cut back or replaced. For example, many couples spend too much time visiting relatives and not enough time with each other. So, schedule some coupling activities and make the time. It's more important than many of the other things you do!

One way to plan coupling activities is to make independent lists of the things you would like to do. Try to make each of your lists as long and as creative as possible. You may even want to work on them over several days so that new ideas can be added as you think of them. Keep working until you each have a *minimum* of ten ideas. Twenty or thirty is better. Then, try combining ideas from each person's list into coupling activities. For example, if Tom has "taking a drive" and "going for a walk in the woods" on his list and Susan has "eating breakfast out" and "taking photographs," they can combine these by going out for breakfast, followed by a drive in the country to a woods where they can go for a walk and take photos. You can also alternate between the two lists. If Susan wants to go to a meeting of the Sierra Club and Tom wants to go cross-country skiing, they can take turns. Coupling activities that are repetitive and have a built-in commitment—for example, a joint class of some sort—are also a good idea, since they happen routinely.

While it is important to plan most coupling activities, it is also a good idea to leave some room for spontaneity. If your partner suggests that you do something on the spur of the moment, give it a try! In most cases, you'll find that you enjoy it too. Willingness to be adventurous and do things spontaneously is important if you are to have more excitement in your life. Take turns seeing who can think up the most zany spur-of-the-moment ideas.

Strictly speaking, doing things with friends isn't the same as coupling, but many couples are lonely, and making friends can be a very good way to overcome this. You may have to show some initiative by inviting other couples over for dinner or dessert, or by organizing joint activities, but the friendships that develop can provide a number of rewards and some new opportunities for coupling. Planning a meal, talking about your friends and their interaction, or driving to their house can all provide nice times together.

A side benefit of coupling activities is that it will revitalize your conversation. As you engage in joint planning of your new activities, you will have lots more to talk about. Anticipating upcoming events or reviewing last week's adventures can enrich your conversations and shift the focus to more pleasant topics.

Being More Affectionate

Increasing the amount of physical affection that you give to your partner can also make a difference. Holding hands, putting your arm around your partner, hugging, cuddling, kissing, stroking your partner's hair, or caressing your partner's arm can all send a message that you care. And affection is an important antidote to conflict.

If you are no longer exchanging affection at all, reintroducing it may seem daunting, but it is not as difficult as you might think. Wait until you are not in conflict and start with something simple, such as taking your partner's hand. If you haven't done this for some time, you can explain that you now want to be more affectionate. Once you have broken the ice, it will be important to gradually increase the amount of affection that you give. Of course, choosing the right occasions and exactly how you want to express your caring must be compatible with your own style, but try to push yourself a bit.

Consider the following: kissing your partner hello and goodbye; holding hands while watching television; having a cuddle before going to sleep; snuggling before you get up in the morning; putting your arm around your partner when you walk down the street; giving your partner a hug for no reason at all; stroking your partner's hair when he or she is driving; or giving your partner a kiss when he or she has done something that pleases you. Coupling activities also provide a good time for affection. Don't worry about overdoing it—for most people, there is no such thing as too much affection.

You can also ask for affection when *you* need it. You can say things like: "Can I have a hug?" or "Let's have a cuddle" or "What about a kiss?" However, this will work only if you have been giving your fair share of affection. Don't expect your partner to be the first to change—instead, accept the responsibility yourself.

Some couples run into problems because they confuse affection with sex. These partners may interpret any sign of affection as a sexual overture—and in some cases they may be right! Affection is part of sex. But sex need not be part of affection. Therefore, it is a good idea to establish affection as something for its own sake—something that says that you care, but that doesn't carry any other expectations. To do this, you may need to make your signals clearer so that simple affection and sexual approaches can be distinguished more easily. The best way to differentiate the two is to use unambiguous verbal requests to initiate sex. For example: "I'd like to make love, are you interested?" or, "I want to have sex with you." Indeed, any clear signal that you are interested in lovemaking should work. Talking this over and finding signals that discriminate will allow you to have lots of affectionate nonverbal interchanges that *don't* confuse sex with affection.

Tell Your Partner That You Care

The expression "I love you" is an important one, but if you get tired of using it, there are countless other ways to say it. A few examples: "I like being with you"; "I care about you"; "It's nice to be together"; "I enjoy you"; "I feel really passionate about you"; "I'm having fun with you"; "You're a great person"; "I'm crazy about you"; "I adore you." When giving verbal affection, be honest. Don't say things you don't feel. But do search for opportunities to say that you care, and use a little imagination! Typically, people don't state their positive feelings strongly enough. Try to give your caring statements some punch.

Endearing names are also fun. Some couples have special nicknames for each other. Others use more common terms, such as "darling"; "baby"; "sweetheart"; and so on. If you don't like any of the standard names, make up your own. One word of caution, though—make sure that your partner likes the term of endearment you've chosen! If it merely annoys your partner, it will do little to improve the positive feelings between you.

Mention Things That You Like

Another way to express your regard is to praise or compliment your partner. Think about all the things that you like about your partner. For example, what do you like about your partner physically? How can you express this? Suppose that you like your partner's hands. Wait for an appropriate moment, such as when you are holding hands, and say something like: "You have the most delicate and beautiful hands"; "I like the shape of your fingernails"; "Your hand feels soft"; or "Your hands are so strong."

What else do you like about your partner's body? Consider everything from the top of the head right down to the toenails, including such things as a well-placed mole or a sexy voice. If you like your partner's hair, what do you like about it? Do you like its color, texture, softness, style, curls, or shine? Chances are there are a number of physical attributes that you can rave about! Don't be afraid to be creative. One husband regularly compared his wife's hair to moonlight and her eyes to deep glacial pools. This may sound corny, but his wife loved it!

If your partner tries a new style or wears something attractive, mention it! "I like your new haircut"; "That blue sweater looks really lovely with your blue eyes"; "You look handsome in that shirt"; "That nightgown really turns me on."

Mention things that your partner does that you like: "I like it when you kiss me that way"; "I really enjoyed dinner"; "When you buy presents for the kids, I really appreciate it"; "That was terrific, the way you got everything so organized"; "I enjoyed the way we made love today." Marriage counselors sometimes call this "Catch your partner doing something you like." Acknowledging the behaviors that you appreciate will also help your partner learn how to please you better, so there are payoffs for you as well.

Next, consider what you like about your partner's personality. Is he or she funny, considerate, gentle, feminine, masculine, assertive, ambitious, hardworking, a good parent, generous, good company, clever, affectionate, or sexy? Think about it until you have identified some characteristics that you admire. Never mind the ones that you don't like—this is an exercise in identifying what you *do* like. The next step is to let your partner know: "I like it when you're funny"; "I enjoy talking to you"; "I admire your cleverness"; "You're so sexy," and so on.

Of course, broader statements of a positive nature don't hurt either. Try telling your partner that he or she is "beautiful," "wonderful," "adorable," "fantastic," "super," "a great person," etc.

Be Romantic

Romantic gestures, surprises, and gifts are another good way to show affection. These can include sending flowers to the office (for both sexes—men like flowers, too); buying

sexy underwear; making a favorite dessert; leaving love messages around the house; putting flowers next to the bed; planning a night out and taking care of all the arrangements;
buying a romantic gift; writing a love letter; making a reser-
vation for a dream holiday just for the two of you; putting together a photo album of happy times; making a Valentine's
Day present; having the bedroom alight with candles; or
bringing your partner a drink in the bath. There are many
more things you can think of, if you use some creativity and
spend a little time at it. Many of these romantic gestures can
be as fun to give as they are to receive.

Looking nice for your partner is another way to increase
the good feelings between you. If you make an effort to look
your best, your partner will be more attracted to you and, in
turn, may try to be more attractive for you. So, exercise, buy
some new clothes, try a new hair style, wear perfume, or buy
some sexy underwear and throw away the worn-out stuff
(men too).

More and Better Sex

More and better sex can also be an antidote to conflict. As
will be discussed in more detail later, your sex life cannot be
separated from the rest of your relationship, and frequent conflict of any type is likely to affect your sexual interaction.
Since it is hard to enjoy sex when you are angry with your
partner, learning to negotiate can have a very beneficial effect
on your sex life.

At the same time, more and better sex can *prevent* unnecessary conflict by lowering the threshold for assuming the worst
and by making you feel more positive toward your partner.
Sometimes couples become irritable and grouchy simply because they are not making love (and having their sexual needs

met) often enough. If you are busy with other pressures and find that the frequency of your lovemaking has dropped off, you may want to devote more time to your sexual relationship.

When couples don't have sex very often, each encounter becomes overly important. This in itself can result in problems. By contrast, having sex more frequently allows couples to get rid of that "all or nothing" feeling and to relax. Most couples find that the more they practice, the more they improve the quality of their sex life. Books such as *Treat Yourself to a Better Sex Life* (see Further Reading) offer suggestions to help you satisfy each other better and to overcome some of the many problems that couples commonly face. So, consider making love more often, and devote a little more energy toward trying to make your lovemaking special. Begin by making the effort to look sexy for your partner. Then set the scene with candles or soft music. Spend some time getting in the mood and warming up before rushing into sexual activities. Let yourself relax and focus on pleasant sensations. Don't allow yourself to become concerned with performance. It doesn't matter whether you perform to some predetermined standard—what is important is that you get maximum enjoyment out of your intimate time together. If concerns or worries occur, dismiss them and concentrate on pleasurable feelings. If you are worrying, you won't be enjoying what's happening. So, let go and enjoy yourself. Finally, when you have finished lovemaking, don't rush away to the shower or turn over and fall asleep. Cuddle for a while and express your positive feelings toward each other. This doesn't mean that you can't sometimes have "quickies" or vary your lovemaking pattern in all sorts of ways. It does mean that you should be careful not to let your lovemaking fall into a dull routine that leaves either partner's needs unmet. So, a little creativity and initiative can go a long way toward improving your sex life. And remember, it's not just up to the man. Women can be creative too. If you find it difficult, think of someone who is very seductive (for example, an actor or actress) and imagine that you are that person. Then think about how he or she would seduce a partner. Next, pretend to be this person and follow through on these behaviors. And since you are no longer "you," you can give up your inhibitions and be more sexually aggressive! If you still need some help, take a look at *The Joy of Sex* and *More Joy of Sex* for some additional ideas (see Further Reading). Sex is a very important form of communication. By giving it some extra attention, you can let your partner know in the most basic way that your relationship *is* important to you. Chapter 19 will discuss what to do if conflict over sex interferes with your ability to relate in this vital area.

Caring Days

As can be seen, there are many things that you can do to make your relationship with your partner more affectionate and caring. But getting started on this is not easy when you are feeling angry, so you may need to work on challenging your angry thoughts before you begin.

Making a list of things to do or say can strengthen your commitment and provide a cue to remind you to follow through on what you have planned. Try to do at least five little positive gestures as a minimum every day. Small, frequent acts of caring convey that you think your partner and your relationship are important. These behaviors will soon become second nature.

Another good way to regularize affectionate behavior is to schedule "caring days." These can be designated as often as you want—weekly or monthly, for example. During a caring day, one partner gives a series of special little surprises and caring gestures to the other without expecting anything in return. Normally, this takes a little planning, which in itself can be fun. When the chosen day arrives, caring gestures should be put into effect regardless of whether the other person is appreciative or grateful. Then, if the other person wishes to, on the following week or month, he or she can reciprocate. Caring days can be fun for both the giver and receiver, and they are a good way to make sure that you are communicating that you care. Be especially careful never to allow caring days to become the subject of a fight. Genuine caring behaviors can never be coerced. Caring days are strictly voluntary and optional, even when they are scheduled.

In summary, you can expect to stay in love only if you give your partner and your relationship the attention they deserve. Feelings of love come from both partners' expressing how much they like each other on a day to day basis. By having enjoyable times together, expressing affection, telling your partner that you care, being romantic, and having more and better sex, you can replace conflict spirals with more positive cooperative spirals. Reverberating echoes of affection and caring are much nicer than tit-for-tat exchanges of anger. If you are still not convinced that giving your partner more positive attention can make a difference, try it—you might find that you like it!

IV

Yes,
But . . .

18

Keeping Outside Pressures Outside Your Relationship

You may have noticed that your ability to get along with your partner is at its worst when you are up to your ears in other pressures. Couples often complain that their relationship deteriorates just when they most need support from each other. This in itself can become a further source of disappointment and resentment, as each partner feels that the other doesn't understand or doesn't want to understand.

Outside pressures have a way of impinging on relationships and taking their toll. When one or both partners are under stress, the relationship can suffer dramatically. A number of factors contribute to this. First, partners who are experiencing outside pressures usually become worried, tired, irritable, and grouchy. Second, there may be less time for relationship maintenance, since energy, both physical and emotional, is being expended outside the relationship. Of course, both of these factors make conflict more likely. But the majority of conflicts occur when problems outside the relationship are converted into problems within the relationship. This tends to happen when partners take responsibility for each other's problems or relinquish responsibility for their own.

When a partner inappropriately takes responsibility for the other person's problems, he or she may offer ill-informed advice, false reassurance, or inappropriate solutions, when what is really desired is an opportunity to complain to a sympathetic listener—and nothing more! This can cause the frustration over the original problem to shift to frustration with the spouse, and an argument may ensue. In other cases, the person with the problem may inappropriately dump angry or depressed feelings onto the spouse, *expecting* the spouse to take responsibility and make him or her feel better. Fortunately, couples can learn how to listen to each other in a supportive manner. This will help a great deal.

When both partners are under pressure at the same time, the dangers are compounded. When such stress is chronic, it becomes difficult, indeed almost impossible, to keep even the best relationship on an even keel.

Jobs are one of the most common sources of outside pressure, but many other things can cause stress, such as debts, elderly parents, school or other problems with the kids, or illness. Some couples have more to deal with than others, but almost all couples have to face one or more periods of severe stress and frequent periods of moderate stress. The strategies discussed in this chapter are general principles that can be applied to most situations. More specific suggestions will be discussed in chapters 19 and 20.

Share Your Problems with Your Partner

The first step in keeping outside pressures from having too great an effect on your relationship is to recognize their existence and to talk them over with your partner. Sharing your worries and concerns is beneficial, because getting them out in the open can help you understand them better. And a sympathetic listener can have a very therapeutic effect. Problems have a way of seeming bigger when you keep them bottled up inside you. Explaining them to another person often clarifies the issues, which makes them seem more manageable. It can also stimulate new ideas for tackling problems. Moreover, knowing that your partner cares enough to listen can help you feel less isolated and alone. And an equally important benefit is that your partner will understand the real reasons behind your upset, so won't inappropriately assume that the problem is between the two of you.

If your spouse is suffering from outside pressures, encourage him or her to talk about them. The best way to let your partner know that you've understood is to engage in active listening, which promotes growth and self-initiated problem solving. Be sure to give your partner your full attention and enough time to tell the whole story. Ask your partner questions about how he or she feels. Then reflect what you have heard, to make sure that you understand and to let your spouse know that you have listened. Accept, rather than try to change, the way your partner feels! Express concern when appropriate; if your partner is really upset, a supportive hug can be much appreciated. Finally, you may want to encourage your partner to review the potential solutions that he or she is considering. Don't expect that all such discussions will end conclusively. Your partner may work it out for him- or herself later, having benefited from talking it over with you.

Be sure, however, to avoid the trap of taking the responsibility for solving your partner's problems. Many people listen to a few minutes of explanation and then hop in with unsolicited advice, offering suggestions about how the other person *should* handle the problem. This can be extremely aggravating to a partner who is already feeling uptight. Not only has the partner been denied the opportunity to blow off steam and complain, but he or she has been offered a hasty, usually ill-conceived solution to a problem that has probably been on his or her mind for some time. Typically, this leads to a debate about the feasibility of the proposed solution. The person who has offered the suggestion may become offended when the attempt to "help" is rejected, and the partner with the problem may feel pressured to come up with his or her own instant alternative or to agree to the other's proposal.

In summary, outside pressures can quickly turn into a conflict between you when you take on responsibility for your partner's problems. So, try to support your partner *without* accepting responsibility for solving all of his or her problems. If your partner asks for suggestions or help, by all means give them or propose a brainstorming session, but don't assume that you know what's right for your partner. Doing so will undermine your spouse's confidence, and you may not understand all of the angles anyway.

Every year, hundreds of thousands of people pay professionals to let them talk through their problems and find their own solutions to the pressures of modern life. Spouses who learn to do this for each other will be providing an important service and building a solid bond of supportiveness and intimacy. And they may even save themselves some money!

Don't Take Your Problems out on Your Family

The second step involves making an effort not to take your problems out on your partner or family. We are all familiar with the cliché about the boss who shouts at the employee, who goes home and shouts at his wife, who then shouts at the kids, who then kick the cat. (Of course, women can begin this process too.) This cliché is popular because it contains an element of truth. The tendency to displace anger and dump problems onto your partner was discussed briefly in chapter 16. Many people seem to believe that if they feel irritable, they have the right to act it out—with whoever is around! But displacing anger onto one's partner or children doesn't solve anything, and it's not only unfair, but it's likely to lead to further conflict and stress.

Indeed, one of the hallmarks of emotional maturity is the ability to assume responsibility for one's own negative feelings. As children, many of us learned to expect someone else to cheer us up, by kissing away the tears or jollying us into a better mood. But our spouses are not our parents, and we are no longer children. One of the common dangers of expecting partners to rescue us from bad moods is that, by making them responsible for making us feel better, we abandon responsibility for ourselves. When your partner doesn't do the "right" thing, he or she becomes a new source of anger for being "insensitive," "unsympathetic," or "not understanding." This is certainly not fair!

As mentioned in the preceding section, tell your spouse your troubles, but don't expect him or her to assume responsibility for cheering you up. That is your own responsibility, and the best way to achieve it is to take control of trying to resolve the problems that are upsetting you.

Taking Responsibility for Your Own Problems

Imagine that you have had a bad day at work. What can you do to take responsibility for your problem and be sure that you don't take it out on your family? Using self-talk is a good way to start. As you drive home from work, think to yourself: "Okay. Tonight I'll try to remember not to be a grouch. Just because I'm upset about work doesn't give me an excuse to take it out on my family. It's not their fault and they shouldn't have to suffer. I'll share what's bothering me with my partner, and then I'll go for a run to let off some steam, so that I can relax and enjoy the rest of the evening."

When you get home, tell your spouse about your troubles, explaining that you are trying to fight off a bad mood and you will try your best not to be grouchy. However, be careful not to use this to get your own way or to bully your family into treating you with kid gloves, since this is just another way of taking it out on the family. Of course, you may not be the only one who had a bad day, so don't forget to listen to your partner's complaints as well.

It is also a good idea to discuss how you will handle the evening to reduce your tension and prevent conflict. For example, you may decide that something special and particularly distracting or relaxing is called for, such as a spontaneous night out, a hot bath, a back rub, or a good night's rest. If you have some special needs, express them as a simple request, but be careful not to demand that the family subordinate their needs to yours. There is a big difference between asking for a back rub and forbidding the kids to watch television because you don't want to hear the noise. So, go for a walk if you don't like the noise—it might do you good! Of course, how you handle the evening can become the subject of a brief negotiation where, for example, it may be possible to exchange peace and quiet for some promised compensation on the weekend.

Work outside the home is not the only source of stress for couples. Work at home can also be very stressful, as any housewife and mother or househusband and father can testify. Sometimes partners seem to believe that because a spouse stays home, he or she has it "easy." In most cases, nothing could be further from the truth. Managing the house and kids can be more stressful and tiring than the most stressful executive job. If you don't believe that, try it for a week! Chances are, you'll be glad to return to your workplace. Of course, failure to recognize this fact can be yet another source of aggravation. So, if your partner has what is euphemistically referred to as "home duties," give some thought to his or her special problems, listen actively to complaints, and offer to help in resolving them. (Note that offering to help is not the same as taking responsibility!)

Do Something About Resolving Your Problems

If stress is ongoing, it is *especially* important that you take control of the problem by doing something about it. Research has repeatedly shown that feeling in control is an important factor in maintaining good mental health and feelings of well-being. Doing something, even if it isn't 100 percent effective, is likely to make you feel better, because you are exerting at least *some* control over the situation.

If the problem involves conflict (for example, conflict at work), consider using the negotiation method, since the model is applicable to all types of conflicts. But even if the problem does not involve conflict, brainstorming may be useful in generating solutions. You can also consult others whom you respect to help generate further ideas. In every situation, there are usually *many* different things you can do. Once you have identified what you consider the best solution, put it into practice. Don't just passively put up with the problem—do something about it! If that doesn't work, try something else. If you have done everything that you can to resolve the problem and it still persists, you may want to consider leaving the situation or seeking professional advice.

Take Time Out from Thinking About Your Problems

In addition to your attempts to resolve the causes of your stress, you may want to employ some strategies to help you cope with stress and to reduce its adverse effects. These strategies should *not*, however, be used as a substitute for trying to resolve the problem. The most important way to manage stress is to remove its source. But since anxiety and unproductive worry will leave you less able to deal effectively with your problems, you may want to exercise some control over your worry, while you work out what to do.

One place to begin is with "thought stopping." This is a simple strategy for managing unnecessary worrying, but becoming good at it requires practice. When you find yourself worrying, simply say to yourself, "Stop!" and then try to think about something else. The idea is to interrupt the worried thoughts and to replace them with more pleasant thoughts or images. Try, for example, to visualize a relaxing scene. Imagine that you are lying on a beach listening to waves beating against the shore. At first, you may find that you return to worrying within a few seconds. If so, simply catch yourself again, tell yourself to stop, and switch your thoughts once more. You may need to do this over and over. Eventually, you will become increasingly successful, but it *will* require practice. After all, you have probably been practicing how to worry for years, so you can't expect to learn how to stop worrying overnight. Thought stopping is a particularly good technique to practice in bed when you are having trouble sleeping.

Think About the Problem Differently

Another way to tackle worrying is to challenge your thoughts. This method was explained in chapter 14, where you were encouraged to challenge your angry thoughts about your partner. This same strategy can be applied to *any* unproductive thoughts, and excessive worrying can certainly be unproductive!

One of the things that people commonly do when they worry about problems or pressures is to "catastrophize." This means to think about the worst things that can happen as if they are likely to happen. As discussed earlier, *how* you think about things can have a big effect on the way you feel and behave. It is not hard to see how you can feel more and more anxious the more you catastrophize. So, replace catastrophizing with more coping thoughts. Tell yourself that you *will* solve this problem and that it's not that important anyway, in the larger scheme of things.

Self-criticism and self-blame are also bad habits that can cause you to feel bad. Many people tend to be their own worst critics. Even if you have not handled a situation as well as you wished you had, chances are that there were reasons for this. In any case, beating yourself over the head seldom helps to remedy the situation but further reduces confidence and undermines your ability to put things right or to handle similar situations in the future. So, challenging undue self-criticism is important too.

Finally, although most people are quick to criticize themselves, they seldom give themselves enough praise. Giving yourself credit is especially important when handling difficult situations. Self-praise is a key to self-confidence, and self-confidence is necessary in trying times. Moreover, giving yourself sufficient self-praise can lessen the stress of an adverse situation by allowing you to accept that, although the situation is difficult, you are doing your best to manage it. Even if you don't feel good about how you handled a situation, try to identify some part of it that you *can* feel good about, and give yourself a pat on the back for doing that part well.

Getting Away from the Problem

Another way to shut out outside pressures is to take time away from them. Engaging in activities that are so absorbing that you can't think of anything else usually works. Exercise or a favorite sport may do this for you. Running, swimming, aerobic dancing, skiing, tennis, squash, golf, and so on may all provide some time out from feeling pressured. Entertainment can also be distracting. Reading an absorbing book, working on a crossword puzzle, or watching something diverting on television can help too.

Getting away from the situation for a while by taking a vacation is even more effective. Often this allows you to get some real distance from the issue and gain a new perspective. And a new perspective may lead to new ideas about how to resolve the problem. Moreover, vacations can also cause you to reassess your priorities and to think about what's really important in your life. If outside pressures have been affecting your relationship, you will have a chance to see this more clearly. And there is a good chance that once you have relaxed and gained some distance from your problems at home, you will find that your relationship has improved.

Remember, it's up to you to do your best to keep outside pressures outside of your relationship. Sharing your problems with your partner can help to put them in perspective and make both of you aware that they are external to your relationship. Moreover, talking about your problems may be therapeutic. Be sure, however, not to place the responsibility on your partner. Instead, take responsibility for your own problems and try to overcome them in ways that don't involve displacing your anger onto those you love. Rethinking the problem, taking active steps to solve it, and finding ways to get a break from it all can help you to do this.

If your spouse has too many outside pressures, you will need to take care not to accept responsibility for trying to solve them. Keep your solutions and unsolicited advice to yourself, and instead concentrate your efforts on becoming a sympathetic listener. Partners who take responsibility for their own problems and resist the urge to try to solve their spouse's problems can avoid many unnecessary disputes and increase their own problem-solving and coping skills in the bargain.

19

Tackling the "Hot" Issues and the Serious Relationship Problems

For many couples, money, sex, and in-laws are the issues that generate the most emotional heat. However, they need not be a continuing source of conflict. Extramarital affairs, alcohol problems, and violence are more serious issues, but they too can be overcome, with professional help if necessary. Although many books have been written about each of these issues, the suggestions listed below may start you thinking about how you can get on top of these problems. Further recommendations can be obtained through additional reading (see Further Reading) or professional help.

Money Hassles

Whether or not money is the root of all evil, it is certainly the root of many marital squabbles. Money seems to cause the most problems when there's not enough of it! Perhaps for this reason, it is a favorite bone of contention for newly married couples—although a dispute over money can rear its ugly head whenever money is in short supply.

Deciding who should spend how much, on what, and when, is an ideal issue for negotiation, since such conflicts are based on differing, clearly defined interests. So, if money is an issue, schedule a negotiation session to create ground rules and to work out a basic budget. This can dramatically reduce future conflict. Unexpected expenditures can then be dealt with under "expenses," "clothes," etc., until you have an exhaustive list. Then go through it together, and write down each person's interests with regard to that item, as shown in the example on page 203. Remember not to interrupt your partner, and to ask questions, so that you can fully understand your partner's interests.

Once you have listed each person's interests for all the budgetary items, go back through and circle the items that one or both of you think are *absolutely* necessary. Don't debate these. If one of you doesn't think an item is essential and the other does, circle it. Then, based on information about your past expenses, try to estimate an average monthly amount to cover each circled item. When these have been added together, add another 10 percent for unforeseen expenses and compare this total to the amount that you have to spend.

If your expenses exceed your income, you will need to do some brainstorming on how you might further reduce essential expenditures or increase your income—even a little. Remember that brainstorming involves a creative flow of ideas, and no ideas should be criticized. Write them all down. Then try to fit ideas together until you can achieve a mutually acceptable solution and a plan for pursuing it. If you are unable to go on to the uncircled interests on your list, you will have to wait until your income increases or you have a windfall. But, having gone through this process, you will at least have a clearer idea of what you can and can't afford and a set of rules to help you avoid conflict. Moreover, you will know what your priorities are when your income does increase.

If, however, your income exceeds your essential expenses, go back over your budget and number the remaining items on your own list of interests in the order of their importance to you. Then, one at a time, go through the items on the list and set an average amount next to each. Keep your estimates reasonable. It is a good idea to let the person whose interest is being discussed suggest the amount to be written down— without argument from the other. Don't worry about trying to equalize the amounts of money for each person—different things make different people happy, and some happen to be more expensive than others. Just write down the amount necessary to fulfill the basic requirements of the interest. Then add the amounts required to fulfill each person's first preference to the total of your basic budget. If your income still exceeds your expenses, go to the second set of preferences, and so on. Of course, through brainstorming you may be able to figure out ways to increase your income.

Negotiating a basic budget in this way will help you establish rules for the essentials, and then, jointly and systematically, work out what extras you can afford. By putting everything on the table—including essentials, extras, and income—you can maximize your chances of achieving the right balance with the opportunities that are open to you, and you will also be more likely to consider all the possibilities. Setting out all the categories of expenditure simultaneously, as well as both sets of interests and priorities, provides a system for allocating priorities. Thus, Susan's need to spend more on clothes so that she will feel attractive can be traded for Tom's need to spend money on golf to help him relax. Having such a system for acceptance of each other's interests at face value rather than debating their legitimacy or quibbling about actual

BUDGETARY INTERESTS

	Susan	Tom
Food	• Wants well-rounded diet for the kids	• Wants well-rounded diet for the kids
	• Wants money for special diet foods to stay slim	• Wants supply of snacks to keep his weight up
		• Wants beer available when he gets home from work
Clothes	• Wants to look stylish	• Wants clothes that look expensive so that his clients will believe that he is doing well
	• Wants to look attractive for Tom	
	• Concerned about the kids having nice clothes so they will fit in with the other kids at school	
Car	• Wants car that is big enough to cart the kids' friends around	• Wants a car that is no more than two years old to maintain status with clients
		• Wants to keep the car well serviced to get the best resale value

amounts of money can allow you to sidestep disagreements. However, if you do become hung up on the amounts of money involved, you can simply split the surplus and agree to use the resultant amount for your most preferred, affordable interests. Of course, agreements are always open to renegotiation, so if your interests change, so can your budget allocation. But remember, it's not fair to complain about an expenditure that you have agreed to! If you're unhappy with the rules, reopen the negotiation to discuss the future, but don't complain about the past.

When couples first attempt to negotiate a budget, they often over- or underestimate some expenses. If you are really serious about establishing a basic budget and/or if this is a frequent source of conflict, you may want to keep records for a few months and schedule further budgetary sessions to go over the records together to compare your estimates to your actual expenditures and to make the necessary adjustments.

Unforeseen expenditures or those that exceed the budgeted amount, should, whenever possible, be the topic of a new negotiation *before* the money is committed. Having a 10 percent contingency fund can help take the pressure off in emergencies (and reduce the likelihood of conflict), for example, when the brakes on the car give out. But having a brief negotiation about this before the money is spent can be a good idea for those who are on a tight budget or who are sensitive about this issue.

Finally, if all else fails, consider going to a financial adviser. These professionals can help you work out a budget that will fit your income. Although many couples resist this recommendation because of its cost, if you choose a reputable counselor, you may save money, as well as avoid conflict, in the long run. Financial advisers are particularly useful if you have serious money problems and need to get back on your feet. Ask your bank manager, a certified public accountant, your local chamber of commerce, or legal aid (if your community has it) for a referral to someone who is reputable and whose charges are affordable.

Sex

Couples in conflict often find that their sexual relationship suffers and that sex becomes just another battleground. This is true both for couples who argue too much and for those who don't argue enough. Anger and resentment about other issues often spill over into the sexual relationship. Indeed, it is exceedingly difficult to be spontaneous and giving when you are harboring anger and resentment. Consequently, learning to negotiate, to handle emotions, and to increase positive interactions should lead to more positive feelings between you and have a beneficial effect on your sex life.

In addition to conflict from other issues intruding into your lovemaking, many couples argue over sex itself—for example, quarreling about how often to have sex, how to please each other, what to do and how to do it, and how to discuss it. Often, the basic interests behind these issues are fear of failure, feelings of inadequacy, or concern over whether the partner really cares. Because sexual issues are so tied up with a person's self-concept, they easily threaten self-esteem. Moreover, despite the supposedly liberated times that we live in, sex is still surrounded by layers of cultural mythology, propaganda, and confusion. To make matters even worse, women and men are trained in ways that are often quite contradictory and incompatible. These factors make it extremely hard to talk about sex openly and constructively. But talk you must, if you are to get anywhere with this most almost universal area of conflict.

Contrary to popular thought, satisfying sex for both partners does *not* just happen "naturally." Learning to have satisfying sex with a partner is a complex communication task that requires coordinating two people's preferences and needs, which in themselves may change from moment to moment. It also requires a variety of movements that interact with the other's responses in a complicated manner. To learn what your partner likes, and to teach him or her what you like, requires time and accurate feedback. The expectation that it will all sort itself out automatically, or the equally pernicious assumption that the male partner is supposed to flawlessly orchestrate the whole sequence, can lead to much frustration and conflict. When sex is not satisfying, partners sometimes blame each other, rather than take the time to master the complexities involved. Most people don't expect that they will be able to ski down a mountain perfectly the first few times they try; expecting to have good sex without knowing the basic principles and without practice is equally unlikely.

Accurate information about human sexuality, especially female sexuality (which tends to be more complicated and less obvious than male sexuality), has only been attained in recent years through the works of Masters and Johnson, Shere Hite, and others. However, many couples are still not fully aware of these findings and are continuing to operate on the basis of outdated, biased, and incorrect information.

Moreover, some people, more often women, have difficulty communicating about sex. Having been taught to leave their pleasure up to the man, who is "supposed" to know everything about sex, they expect him to know what to do. Women often fear that showing the man what they want or correcting his moves will offend him. When this fear of hurting the male ego is added to the fact that many women have been trained to feel uncomfortable, embarrassed, and even inhibited about sex, and have been told that it is selfish, greedy, or unladylike to ask for what they need, it is not surprising that so many women have difficulty telling or showing their partner what to do. Finally, some women fear that their partner will wonder how they have learned what they want, since it is still taboo in some sections of society for women to admit that they masturbate or that they have had sex with other partners. And, of course, some women actually do not know what they want and will have to learn.

Unfortunately, this difficulty in communicating puts a terrible strain on both women and men. Many women don't get the stimulation that they need, and their frustration is compounded by their inability to overcome their inhibitions about discussing it. Men may experience a sense of failure or be deprived of the pleasure of completely satisfying their partner. It is no wonder that conflicts occur, as needs (to be satisfied and to satisfy) are left unmet.

Because sexual performance issues are so wrapped up with those of personal identity and sexuality, partners often feel particularly sensitive and vulnerable in this area. Thus, even when they do try to communicate, they may end up arguing. Such conflict merely clouds communication further, as each partner comes to believe that the other person thinks that he or she is inadequate. Hence, instead of gradually improving their sexual understanding and skills over time, some couples find that their sexual relationship deteriorates, as conflict about sex continually erodes their self-confidence and self-esteem.

If you have conflict over sex, you may want to consider using the negotiation model, just as you would with any other issue. If you are having trouble communicating about sex, start with a meta-negotiation. You can begin by discussing how to make talking about sex more comfortable before you go on to talk about sex itself.

If you already do talk about sex but there are some particular issues over which you have conflict—for example, one of you wants to have sex more often than the other—begin by clearly defining the issue to be negotiated. If there is more than one issue, keep them separate and negotiate each one on its own.

If you are having trouble identifying the issues that need to be discussed, ask some preliminary questions to ascertain what you have in common and where you differ. Ask yourselves: "What do we like that we are already doing?" "Is there anything that we do that we want more of?" "Is there anything else that we want more of?" "Is there anything that we are doing that we want less of?" "Is there anything that we are doing that we wish we were doing differently?" "What would we like to change?" Take turns talking about these until you have clarified what the issues are.

Then, sit down side by side at a time when you are not likely to be interrupted. Don't negotiate when you are angry, and don't mix this topic with others. Try to list your interests. You may find that talking about sex is somewhat more emotion-laden than other topics you have negotiated, so be on guard to use your new skills for controlling your own and your partner's emotions. Be sure to listen carefully when your partner is talking and to ask clarifying questions rather than respond defensively. Try to put yourself in your partner's shoes and see things from his or her perspective. Write down your spouse's interests and summarize them when he or she finishes, until you are certain that you have stated all of them correctly. Then, explore your own interests. Remember, it is very important to dig down deep to explore the underlying interests behind the more superficial ones. Even if you find it difficult, keep going. You will feel better once you have fully aired your concerns. Then, generate some creative ideas. If you are persistent, you should be able to generate a number of options.

Accurate information can be helpful at this stage. *Treat Yourself to a Better Sex Life* (see Further Reading) is one of the books that you may want to refer to for help. If you want further information, consult the other books listed in that section.

In addition to talking about sex during negotiation sessions, you will need to learn how to talk about sex *while* you are making love. For the reasons discussed above, this can be difficult, but it will become easier with practice. Use the principles already discussed for making requests. Focus on what you want, be positive and specific, and put your request in "I" language: "I'd like to try the position where I'm on top," or, "I want you to caress my clitoris slowly and gently." Because of embarrassment, the tendency is to give feedback of a negative kind: "I'm tired of this position," or, "You're being too rough." But this kind of feedback can cause your partner to feel criticized and to react defensively. At a minimum, try to indicate your desires by directing your partner with your hand.

One way to become more comfortable with asking for what you want is to rehearse, when you are by yourself. Think about how you would say what you want, and then say it aloud over and over, until you feel bored with the task. This kind of practice is a good way to learn new behavior and to overcome inhibitions.

Partners will also need to be open to direction and to accept it without feeling defensive. If you find that you are reading feedback as criticism, challenge your self-talk. Instead of thinking: "I'm doing this wrong. She thinks I'm inadequate," tell yourself, "She wants our sexual relationship to be good and she's doing her best to tell me what she likes."

If your partner is having trouble telling you what he or she wants, don't be afraid to ask. "How are you enjoying this? Is there anything that you'd prefer? Would you like it better slower, faster, higher, lower, softer, harder . . . ?" Asking often makes it easier for the other person to respond, and the answer will provide you with the feedback you need.

This section has discussed only one of the many problems that couples have in lovemaking. Others, such as problems with achieving orgasm, painful or difficult intercourse, and problems with erection or ejaculation can be tackled by using techniques worked out specifically for these issues. These can be learned through books such as *Treat Yourself to a Better Sex Life*, mentioned above, which provides a self-help guide to the treatment of common sexual problems. If you want to seek professional help, contact a mental health clinic, university psychology clinic, or your doctor for a referral. Many couples find that problems they have lived with for years can be resolved rapidly if both partners attend therapy and follow the recommendations.

Handling the In-Laws

Although many partners and their parents get along fine, learning how to deal with both your own and your partner's parents can be tricky business—no matter how well-intentioned everyone is. In fact, sometimes parents who are the most well-intentioned cause the most problems. There is an almost infinite variety of in-law problems.

One of the most common of these is the demanding or overnurturing parent who has never really separated from the child. Typically, these parents set up the son or daughter to feel caught in a no-win situation between the parents' wishes and the spouse's wishes—much as Tom felt about his and Susan's vacation plan. If he pleases one, he offends the other, and vice versa. The spouse, on the other hand, is placed in a constant power struggle with the in-laws. The frustrated partners often end up in conflict with each other over this un-happy situation. The only real way out of the trap is for the person who is being pulled in two directions to join forces with the spouse and agree to limit the parents' demands to a more reasonable and mutually acceptable level.

Achieving this will give you an opportunity to use your as-sertion skills, especially the ability to say "no." Of course, this is unlikely to be popular with parents at first, and they may even try some coercive strategies or dirty tricks to try to force you to back down. A favorite is the parental guilt game: "How could you do this after all the sacrifices I've made for you?" or variations thereof. This is a powerful ploy, but if you can handle your emotions and ignore it, the behavior will fade. The ideas for sidestepping dirty tricks, which were discussed earlier, will work with parents too. If you set some limits and stick to them, in spite of any coercive tactics that they may try, your parents will likely adjust to the new rules and learn to operate within them. In any case, it is usually healthier for everybody involved when parents learn to find their own sources of happiness without relying entirely on their children or grandchildren. Best of all, such a change is likely to lower the amount of conflict between you and your spouse and make the times when you interact with your parents more re-laxed and pleasant.

Another variation is parents who try to do too much—such as give you money that you don't want, fix things around your house when you haven't asked them to, or buy things for you that you don't need. These parents are usually well-meaning but highly irritating. Typically, they still see you in a depen-dent and childlike role. By using your assertion skills you may be able to set some new rules: "Dad, I'd like to negotiate a solution to a problem that is bothering me. It really upsets me when you come over and fix things around the house without my asking you to. I'd prefer it if you wouldn't do this unless I ask. I realize that you're doing it because you want to help out, and I appreciate that. But I'd like us to make an agreement that if I need some help, I'll feel free to ask you. Could we do that?" Appropriate assertion of this type will usually help. If your parent doesn't listen, repeat yourself. This technique, known as the "broken record," can be very useful in getting your message heard.

Parents and in-laws who tell you how to do things or criticize the way you do them can also be a problem. With in-laws, it is often the mother-in-law who tells the daughter-in-law how to do something. Such highly aggravating behavior must be stopped. Discuss the problem with your partner so that you both have a clear idea of the specific behaviors in question. Try to avoid the temptation to blame your spouse for his or her parents' behavior, and try to resist the urge to be defensive when discussing your parents—after all, you're not responsible for how your parents act. Moreover, don't compare your parents ("*My* mother would never do that"). Instead, work together to write out a specific request for change. Keep improving it until you are satisfied that it is clear, specific, positive, and defines the desired future behavior. It is best for the person whose parents are involved to be the one to make the request for change. For example, after discussion with Susan, Tom made the following request: "Mom, Susan and I feel upset when you criticize us for the way we discipline the kids. In the future, we'd prefer it if you didn't say anything when one of us disciplines the children." Susan told her mother: "When you and Dad insist that we come there for Christmas, we feel caught in the middle between you and Tom's parents, who also insist. In the future, I'd prefer it if you invited us to visit whenever you want us, but if you would also understand that some years we will need to have Christmas with Tom's parents and some years we will want to celebrate by ourselves."

Of course, the skills outlined in this book can also be applied to conflicts with parents and other relatives. But in these kinds of situations, more than one layer of conflict may exist—a first layer of conflict between you and your partner and a second layer between you and the relatives. Therefore, the best way to proceed is to use a two-stage negotiation by reaching a negotiated agreement between the two of you in the first instance, and then working from this plan to negotiate and/or be assertive with your relatives in turn.

When you form your own family, your relationship with your parents will necessarily change. But it is common for your parents to have some trouble adjusting to these changes. When parents become a source of conflict between you and your spouse, the problem can usually be overcome by listening carefully to your spouse's interests and by finding a solution that the two of you can live with. If you do try to redefine the rules, your parents will be able to adapt (even if they protest at first) and you will probably be surprised to find that in the long run, everyone will benefit.

Extramarital Affairs

While a small percentage of couples agree that it is permissible to have sexual relations with people outside their relationship, most people in our society still believe in monogamy—if not for themselves, at least for their spouses!

In relationships where monogamy is an agreed-upon principle, violation of this principle can cause considerable anger, bitterness, and argument—for some time afterward. In fact, infidelity is one of the most common precipitants of relationship breakdown. Whether affairs are a cause or an effect of relationship problems remains a source of debate. However, either way, they have huge potential for conflict. Consequently, this is a clear case of an ounce of prevention being worth a pound of cure. Affairs are easy to become involved in, but they can be extremely difficult and painful to end. So, it is a good idea to think ahead. Violating your contract with your partner may lead to all sorts of unexpected adverse consequences—even if your partner never finds out. You may think that you won't feel guilty, but you probably will. You may think that it won't affect your relationship, but it undoubtedly will. You may think that your partner won't find out, but he or she might, and so on. So, if you have agreed to be monogamous, the best rule is to stick to your agreement or to renegotiate. Of course, many couples do not renegotiate because they fear that even bringing up such a sensitive topic would cause considerable anger and resentment.

Indeed, most people in most relationships do find themselves tempted from time to time. Just because you are married or living with someone doesn't mean that you suddenly stop being attracted to other people. It is not uncommon to have periods of feeling infatuated with someone other than your partner. This has probably happened to you and to your partner as well. Moreover, it is not inconsistent to feel this way and to love your partner at the same time. It's what you do with the infatuation that determines how it affects your relationship.

Of course, people do have affairs and many couples face the task of coming to terms with their feelings when the partner finds out. There are many variations in the way such a conflict impacts on a couple, but a few generalizations can be made. One is that emotions are likely to be intense, and both parties may find themselves feeling temporarily overwhelmed. Applying the suggestions in this book for handling emotions and reexamining your thinking can help you keep these feelings from defeating you. The good news is that all emotions lessen over time, and that no matter how upset you may be at first, you *will* eventually get over it!

No matter how difficult it may be, this is an essential time to use your negotiation skills. It is a time when many aspects of your relationship may need to be renegotiated. In some cases, negotiation may even involve whether you want your relationship to continue.

Not all couples survive with their relationship intact. Sometimes the strains are too great, and one or both parties may not be able to overcome their anger sufficiently. Occasionally (although less often than most people suppose), the spouse may go off with the new person. The problem then becomes how to handle separation with the least amount of trauma. (See chapter 21.)

However, if you do try to rebuild your relationship, it will be important to do so without the confusion, hurt, and anger that an ongoing affair can cause. Almost all marriage counselors agree that it is virtually impossible to rebuild a relationship between two people when three people (or sometimes more) are involved. So, if you are serious about rebuilding a relationship with your spouse, you will need to devote all your resources to this task and say goodbye to the other person in your life.

Often it is the partner who did not have the affair who takes the longest to recover, who is most likely to feel like the loser, and who keeps the conflict going because of feelings of hurt and perceptions of imbalance. How this partner thinks about the affair can affect, at least in part, the speed with which the relationship mends. Partners in this situation commonly dwell on the perceived betrayal or torture themselves by mulling over the gory details (real or imagined). Often they make the (usually false) assumption that if their spouse had an affair, it must mean that he or she no longer cares for them.

These unhelpful thoughts can be replaced by more useful self-talk. If you are in this situation, use thought stopping to switch off unproductive and hurtful replays of the details. Tell yourself that although you don't like what has happened, you *can* cope; do *not* tell yourself that it is the most dreadful thing that ever happened and you can't cope. Remind yourself that most people have the capacity to love more than one person, much as parents do when they learn to love a second child without their love for the first child being diminished. Finally, tell yourself that you and your partner can rebuild your relationship and learn from this situation.

This can even be a good time to correct many of the past problems in your relationship and to start over with more constructive relationship rules and principles. However, it will also be a time to be particularly wary of power struggles. Indeed, in some cases, the person who had the affair may emerge with increased power if the spouse, fearing that the other is less committed, concedes to the other's wishes in a bid to please. Threats to continue the affair or comparisons between the other person and the partner are definitely in the category of dirty tricks and should not be tolerated. In other instances, the person who did not have the affair may end up with increased power, through the invocation of guilt or threats of reprisal. But such tactics will not work to gain an advantage in the long run, since they are basically coercive.

Once again, it is best to use the negotiation method. It is important to be constructive and to follow the model, rather than succumb to complaining and cross-complaining. Remember that feelings will be raw, so mutual respect and caring for each other is especially important at this time. Also be sure to give yourself plenty of time. Renegotiating your relationship and overcoming the natural feelings of hurt and anger may take months or even years. So, take your time and get your relationship rules right.

Although extramarital affairs can be the source of some of the most intense conflict, partners can and do recover and rebuild solid, intimate relationships. But how you choose to handle the conflict can be important in determining whether you will make it. Renegotiating your relationship may be a painful task, but, like tempered steel, relationships that have been through the fire and survived may end up stronger.

Problem Drinking

The most common type of drug abuse is excessive drinking, and one or both partners may have this problem. While a drinking problem can be a response to other relationship problems, it can also exacerbate them. Feelings of anger or resentment may emerge without restraint when one or both partners have had too much to drink. This is because alcohol sometimes acts to disinhibit emotions. Hence, arguments under the influence of alcohol often turn nasty.

Since overdrinking is sometimes used as a way to cope with other problems, working out more acceptable solutions to those problems may result in the person automatically drinking less. In other cases, however, the drinking problem itself must be dealt with.

There are two schools of thought in the treatment of problem drinking. One suggests that total abstinence is required. Alcoholics Anonymous, an example of this approach, is still one of the most successful treatments for people with serious drinking problems. The other approach suggests that heavy drinkers can learn to become "controlled drinkers" by setting drinking goals, by finding other sources of pleasure, and by finding other ways to deal with problems. Many behavioral psychologists espouse the second theory and teach people how to gain control of their drinking problems by learning new habits.

If you are seeking treatment, consider which approach would work best for you, then call your doctor, a psychologist, or the nearest mental health clinic and ask for a referral to an appropriate service.

In any case, if you are really serious about working on your relationship problems and if alcohol is a factor in your conflicts, it is important to do something about it, whether you do it on your own or with professional help.

If contentious topics do come up when you or your partner have had too much to drink, reschedule them for a time when you are not under the influence, so that you can be more rational and keep your emotions under control. And never schedule negotiation sessions for times when you will be drinking heavily.

Family Violence

Physical violence within intimate relationships is more common than most of us like to think. Much of it involves men using violence against women, but a small proportion is perpetrated by women against men. In some couples, both engage in physical violence during the heat of battle. Often, those who become physically violent had parents who did the same thing, teaching them this method for handling intense anger or frustration. Nonetheless, since people are fragile, the use of violence is dangerous—both physically and psychologically. The number of adults and children who are injured, sometimes seriously, from domestic violence is staggering. Physical violence is also damaging psychologically for the victim, the perpetrator, and their children. *Nobody wins when arguments turn violent!* If your partner does become violent, be careful not to provoke him or her further. You will need to do your best to control your own anger, as this is an especially important time to put into practice the suggestions for controlling emotions. Then, when things have calmed down, ask your partner to seek professional help and offer to take part in the search for the right assistance. Your partner may be more willing to go to therapy if you offer to accompany him or her.

Physical violence is *never* a good method for handling anger or conflict. There are much better ways to manage conflict that make everyone happier, including the person who is prone to use physical violence. Fortunately, these more constructive ways can be learned. So, if physical violence is a problem in your relationship, seek help as soon as possible. There is no need to feel ashamed or embarrassed about getting professional help. The important thing is not what you have done in the past. The important issue is what you are trying to do to make the future better. So, call a psychologist, mental health clinic, social worker or doctor to get a referral to someone who can teach you better anger management. The person you are referred to will not be judgmental and will be able to offer you some new skills to replace the behaviors that you have used in the past. Gaining control of your emotional impulses can be a very rewarding experience that increases your feelings of self-esteem. Equally important, your family will also benefit.

Finally, if you are a victim of physical violence and you can't persuade your partner to seek help, you may wish to give serious consideration to staying in the relationship. If your partner is so unwilling to change, you (and possibly your children) may be at risk. However, if you decide to leave a violent partner, it is best to do so in a planned manner and when things are calm. It is also a good idea to get assistance from family, friends, a social worker, or the police to ensure that the separation occurs with minimal fuss. Most communities now have refuges and shelters for women and children who have nowhere else to go. If you are afraid of your spouse, you can also get a restraining order from the courts, which means that your spouse doesn't have the right to visit. If despite such a court order your partner still tries to bother you, he will be subject to arrest.

Although the relationship problems discussed in this chapter can be the source of much heated debate and some of them can present serious problems, all of them can be tackled and overcome. Determination to conquer your problems—whatever they are—can signal an important commitment to your relationship. Actively taking control to make things better, rather than passively allowing things to deteriorate, will give your relationship an injection of optimism and energy that will help you to overcome even the most intractable problems. So, give it your best—it's the *only* way to succeed!

20

Renegotiating Relationship Roles

Changes in circumstances usually require an overhaul of relationship rules, especially when the change affects previously defined roles—for example, when a child is born or when a couple retires. Even changes in the environment, such as moving or changing jobs, may require considerable renegotiation, if conflict is to be handled constructively. Renegotiation may also be needed when circumstances change for one partner, especially when the change has consequences for the relationship, for example when one partner falls ill or becomes unemployed. Because each partner is in a quite different situation, each may have difficulty understanding the other's new interests. The fact that many relationships get into trouble at these critical times suggests the importance of carefully reconsidering both party's needs and concerns and working from these to build creative solutions to address them.

Living Together

Normally, the first time that roles have to be renegotiated is when partners move in together. Differences in preferences and habits quickly become apparent. Many couples report that the first few years of living together were the stormiest of their relationship—and it's no wonder! There are myriad differences that will lead to conflict if the couple doesn't know how to negotiate. These range from trivial decisions, such as which brand of toothpaste to buy, to major ones, such as when to have children or how often to make love. Couples who learn the basic skills of negotiation before they begin living together have a much easier time. Couples who don't, waste a considerable amount of time trying to resolve their problems inappropriately. Opposing fighting styles become well rehearsed and entrenched, making them harder to change later. Runaway escalation and the use of dirty tricks cause much pain and can put the relationship through trying times. That so many couples make it through these traumatic years is a real tribute to the strength of their relationships.

If you and your partner are one of the fortunate couples who do know about negotiation skills from the beginning of your relationship, don't wait around to see if you need them before putting them into effect! Every couple needs negotiation skills. Use them preventively, right from the beginning, and both you and your relationship will be the winners.

When Kids Arrive

The changes brought on by the arrival of a child are enormous. However, apart from getting things ready for the baby, most couples do little to prepare. In fact, the full impact that this event will have on their lives is rarely recognized, and as a result, many couples are in for a shock. The stressfulness of this situation is demonstrated by the fact that it is extremely common for couples coming into therapy to date their marital problems to the time of their first child's birth.

Taking care of a baby, especially for the first couple of years, is an incredibly demanding task that requires one or both of you to give up many of the things that you previously enjoyed. No matter how much pleasure you receive from parenthood, the tasks involved are not *all* pleasant—getting up in the middle of the night when you're dead tired or changing a diaper seemingly for the hundredth time in one day. So, major changes are in store for one or both of you, and it will require serious negotiation to arrive at the best win-win solutions possible.

Negotiating over how you will divide up responsibilities for the care of the baby and how you will reapportion other tasks will be likely to get back to the issues about how you wish to define sex roles, as discussed in chapter 4. If you have a conflict over these definitions, it's especially important to deal with it at the outset, by spending as many sessions of comprehensive negotiation as necessary to fully explore each of your needs and concerns and to develop some creative solutions to your differences. Careful attention will need to be given to the handling of emotions in order to keep the negotiation sessions on track. Be sure to follow the suggestions closely and not to forget to record each step of the negotiation, as outlined.

Indeed, the more of these problems you are able to solve *before* the baby arrives, the further ahead you will be. However, you should still anticipate unpredictable problems, which will have to be tackled as they arise.

Changing Environments—Home or Job

The prospect of moving to a new home is often a source of relationship conflict. Spouses frequently have different perspectives on moving and may even be conflicted within themselves. This occurs because any major change in environment entails some gains and some losses. A decision to move implies that the gains are perceived to outweigh the losses. But when two people are involved, they will inevitably have different assessments of those gains and losses. And the greater the distance involved, the more will be lost in terms of familiarity, friends, and so on.

If couples do not take the time to negotiate, one partner may end up feeling that he or she was forced to move. Alternatively, if the couple does not move, one partner may feel resentful about losing a good opportunity. Such a win-lose outcome can become the source of a long-standing grudge and a sense of inequality in the power balance, based on a feeling of injustice because one's own needs were not adequately considered. As discussed earlier, this kind of resentment can become the source for a host of subsequent everyday conflicts.

Once again, adequate negotiation *before* a decision is made is essential in preventing future conflict. Understanding your own and your partner's needs and concerns will help you more fully evaluate the issue and the real gains and losses involved for each of you. Brainstorming creative options and constructing win-win solutions become particularly important if both parties' needs are to be met.

If you reach a win-win solution that results in moving, the changes involved in the move itself, and in adjusting to the new environment, will require continued negotiation. Any major change is stressful, and the act of moving will require many unforeseeable adjustments. Many people experience a sense of loss—of possessions, places, memories, and friends. In addition, there are usually a number of hassles involved in sorting, packing, and organizing the move, often without adequate time to get everything done. Finally, there is a new environment to adapt to, with new demands, unfamiliar surroundings, and new routines.

In the process of these changes, many decisions need to be made. So, it is important to be alert to the many potential areas for conflict, and to use the negotiation model as a means of arriving at the necessary decisions. Both comprehensive and brief negotiations will need to be frequent, until you have settled into a routine and stabilized your new life to your mutual satisfaction.

Beginning a new job is also stressful. Although it may seem that a change of job affects primarily the partner involved, it can also affect the relationship. This fact sometimes goes unrecognized. But a change in employment can affect the family's income, the amount of free time the employed person has available for the family, the daily routine, and the family's sense of security or status. It can also be compounded by a move to a new home. As discussed above, the more change involved, the more potential for conflict. Therefore, it is equally important to negotiate changes in employment—even if it seems that only one of you is involved. Sharing fears and concerns is especially important, and building ways to address these concerns in your solutions is the only real way to alleviate these difficulties.

Although negotiating about the initial decision is important, it is also important to continue negotiating during the first few months of change, since new jobs are always somewhat unpredictable in terms of the problems that they will present for the relationship. It is important to be sensitive to these changes and to negotiate any issues that have potential for conflict. For example, a new job may necessitate a new routine in the morning—the partners may have to get up at different times; morning chores may need to be divided differently; new arrangements may have to be made for getting the kids to school; transportation to work may require some new accommodation, and so on. If you discuss these changes at your regularly scheduled negotiation sessions and plan how you will handle them, you will be likely to prevent many arguments and considerable stress on your relationship.

Unemployment

When a partner who is accustomed to working becomes unemployed, it can be exceedingly stressful for a couple or family, particularly if the situation goes on for long. For one thing, financial pressures may build rapidly. But other factors affect the situation as well. The partner who is unemployed may at first search for a new job with determination. But if one is not forthcoming, he or she may begin to suffer a loss in self-confidence. The lack of structure and the feelings of failure can add to the loss in self-esteem. In our workaholic culture, not being employed is often seen as a failure, even though the economy is actually programmed for less than full employment. Thus, the unemployed person may not only experience feelings of failure but may actually be perceived to be a failure by others. Unfortunately, this creates a vicious cycle in which loss of self-confidence leads the person to avoid situations where failure is possible. Hence, efforts to find employment may slacken as self-confidence ebbs and depression grows.

As the partner sees the unemployed person losing self-confidence and becoming depressed, the partner may urge the unemployed person to "try harder," in the hope that he or she will eventually find employment and things will return to normal. Further, the partner may believe that the family is also suffering and may feel the burden of being solely responsible for providing the family's income. Thus, the partner may feel a right, or even a duty, to help the unemployed person get out of the doldrums and find a job.

This is a perfect formula for conflict—partners in different situations who don't understand each other's needs and concerns. The best way to tackle this situation is to sit down together and, using the skills you have learned, discuss both parties' interests. After all, it is a shared or joint problem, since both of you, and your children (if you have them), will be suffering. Sharing the problem and then attempting to find a solution can be very comforting for both partners. Brainstorming may provide new ideas. In fact, weekly negotiation sessions on this topic may be useful until the unemployed person finds a job or until some other satisfactory accommodation to the unemployment situation has been found. A single negotiation session can't be expected to solve such a complex problem. Of course, you may also need to practice handling emotions when you first begin to negotiate on this topic, but as you become more accustomed to problem solving rather than arguing, it will become easier. So, tackle the issue together instead of tackling each other, and part of the problem will already be solved.

When Kids Leave Home

Couples may also have to make some role adjustments when children leave home. The "empty nest syndrome" is the term used to describe the plight of women who have stayed home with the children and who are suddenly faced with the loss of a well-established role. In fact, mothers are sometimes faced with a minor version of this role change when the children go to school for the first time. Of course, such changes also affect fathers, but usually less directly, unless they have been the primary caregivers.

When one or more children move away from home, the resulting changes usually require renegotiation. This is a common time for women who have devoted themselves to child rearing to either become depressed (due to their loss of role) or to take up new interests, find a new career, or resume an old one. New needs, wants, fears, and concerns that the female may experience in relation to this new stage in her life will require extended exploration, and may also create new needs, wants, fears, and concerns in her husband as well, all of which need to be addressed. Thorough discussion of these issues, as they arise, can provide a sound basis for understanding and for brainstorming creative options so that win-win solutions can be achieved. Since new roles usually take a while to evolve, negotiation may need to continue for some time, and whenever differences occur.

Retirement

Most couples think of retirement as a time to look forward to, a time when everything will be wonderful. What they may not realize is that this adjustment period can be the source of considerable disillusionment and conflict. No matter what you have planned for your retirement, it is likely to be very different from your previous lifestyle. The myriad deadlines, demands, and short- and long-term goals that you faced in your job(s) will disappear. Suddenly, the rigid structure, which was your life, will change to a complete lack of structure. That may sound wonderful, but, if you are like most people, it will probably require quite a lot of getting used to, and in the meantime you are likely to feel a bit lost. In fact, you may feel very lost, and this will be made worse by your disappointed expectation that everything was going to be great.

In addition, for the first time in your life (except for short periods when you were on vacation), you will be spending every day with your partner. Different habits that you and your partner have developed over the years may suddenly clash, causing conflict.

So, if ever there was a need for good negotiation and planning skills, this is it. Instead of squabbling endlessly, as many newly retired couples do, begin some serious renegotiation about the future and your new roles within the relationship.

Since there is so much to be renegotiated in the early stages of retirement, it may be necessary to increase your negotiation sessions from once a week to twice, or even daily.

In addition, the sooner you find new and enjoyable activities to fill your time, the better off you will be. So, planning is important. Some people think of retirement as sitting back and never doing anything again, but this is a sure formula for unhappiness. Everybody needs to do things that are either goal-oriented, meaningful, or enjoyable, if they are to maintain their mental equilibrium. Retirement provides you with the opportunity to invent and tackle goals that you never had time for in the past. Because some may be individual goals while others may be joint ones, planning may require extra negotiation.

So, study up on your negotiation skills and put them into practice. Remember, the better you are at negotiating and planning, the closer you'll come to achieving that dream of an idyllic retirement.

Illness and Disability

When one partner becomes disabled or chronically ill, an enormous strain is placed on the relationship. A couple's capacity to handle this stressful situation will differ according to the nature of the problem, the coping resources of the partners, and their social support network.

Typically, responsibilities and duties will shift from the ill or disabled partner to the healthy partner or to the children. Sometimes the added weight of responsibility, or the sheer physical activity needed to look after everything, can cause the healthy partner to feel overwhelmed, depressed, and irritable. In addition, the positive day-to-day interactions and rewards from the relationship will probably be reduced, in some cases dramatically so, as a whole range of activities becomes curtailed. The couple may no longer be able to do many of the things they enjoyed, such as going out together, making love, and so on. Naturally, these changes can also take their toll. Moreover, the illness or disability can have significant consequences for the couple's long-term plans and dreams.

The range of activities of the unwell partner may be severely impaired. Old sources of pleasure or achievement will disappear. Illness or disability can also cause all sorts of painful or troublesome physical symptoms. Uncertainty and loss of control may be a further source of anxiety, irritability, and depression.

These are only a few of the many factors that impinge on the family and require adjustment. Of course, in some instances, the illness or disability may also change over time, which can require further adjustment. It is no wonder that partners feel stressed and that this stress often spills over onto the relationship and erupts into conflict.

Conflict that occurs when one partner is ill often has an added dimension, since both partners may feel guilty about the conflict. The healthy partner may feel guilty about his or her anger, because, after all, the illness and its effects are not the ill partner's fault. The ill partner may feel guilty about feeling angry, because the healthy partner has had to give up a normal life and take on many more of the family responsibilities. Therefore, partners are often in a special double bind—they may be frustrated and angry, but when they express their feelings, it leads to argument, and then they feel even more guilty.

As in other changed circumstances, there need to be adjustments in your relationship, and arriving at win-win solutions within the constraints of the situation is especially important. Of course, if your partner is extremely ill or seriously disabled, he or she may not be able to engage in negotiation. In this situation, you can go through the steps of the process on your own. If your partner is unable to explain his or her interests, you may have to do your best to imagine what they may be. Then, you can still brainstorm creative ideas and attempt to arrive at solutions that will meet both of your needs.

In most situations, however, partners are still able to negotiate, and this is a critical time to understand each other's interests. One of the problems is that you are in very different situations, and it may be especially difficult to take each other's role and to fully appreciate how each other feels. This is why the communication of interests is so important. Only through communication will you gain a full realization of what it's like for your partner.

Changing circumstances will almost always require a major review and renegotiation of your relationship rules, and you will need to be aware of this, so that you can devote enough time to it. Returning to formal negotiation sessions at these times is the best way to proceed. Joining together to avoid conflict can help you overcome some of the stress that change naturally creates. Successfully negotiating your relationship through the potential crises that all couples face will help your relationship to survive and thrive.

21

Seeking Help from
a Third Party

The aim of this book has been to help you manage conflict in
your most intimate interpersonal relationship. As you've been
warned, this will take time, effort, and patience. While some
couples feel comfortable learning these skills on their own,
others feel the need for professional help and direction. If you
decide that you are in the latter category, you may wish to
consider marital counseling.

Such counseling can take many different forms; however,
one common element is that *both* of you will need to attend
therapy sessions. Sometimes partners don't discuss their desire to seek marital counseling because they assume (through
an attempt at mind reading) that their spouse won't be interested. When these partners do finally bring it up, they often
find, to their surprise, that their spouse is willing, after all.

If you'd like to try counseling, make a simple request and
see how your partner responds. If he or she has reservations,
schedule the topic for negotiation to further explore your own

and your partner's interests. If you don't reach a win-win solution, you can, of course, reiterate your interests and ask again. Another reason for hesitation is that couples sometimes feel that their marriage has to be in real strife before they seek counseling. In fact, the opposite is true. It is best to seek help *before* your relationship is in deep trouble. In most cases, more progress can be made if you work on problems in a preventive manner, rather than waiting until they snowball out of control. Moreover, successful marital therapy may be shorter and more satisfying if you seek assistance earlier, rather than later.

Getting Rid of Fears About Marital Therapy

Partners who refuse marital counseling usually do so because of fears or concerns. Some of the most common are the fear of being blamed; fear that the therapist will "take sides"; concern or embarrassment about discussing private issues, such as sex; fear of change; and, finally, fear that discussion of the problems will precipitate a complete breakdown in the relationship. Talking over these fears and brainstorming ideas for overcoming them can often clear the air and ease concerns.

A little information about marital therapy may also help to allay fears. Sometimes one partner drags the other along to therapy, firmly believing that the problems in the relationship are all the other person's fault and expecting the therapist to "fix" him or her. But most therapists don't believe that either partner is "at fault." They believe that problems in relationships are due to faulty learning and faulty communication. Thus, in marital therapy, no one is blamed or held responsible. Instead, couples are taught how to communicate more clearly, how to listen, and how to use problem solving and negotiation to resolve their differences.

Contrary to what some people think, therapists *can't* read people's minds (just as partners can't). Rather, they have to rely on what they are told and on what they observe. If you don't want to divulge certain information, you don't have to. But therapists are trained to respond sensitively to personal issues, and most clients find that they quickly feel quite comfortable talking about deeply personal difficulties, including sexual problems.

If you are not satisfied with therapy, you can always go somewhere else. Different therapists have different approaches, and some are more skilled or knowledgeable than others. So, be a discriminating consumer and get what you want. You *can* be in control of the situation at all times. Often this realization makes partners more comfortable about seeking professional help. They can then find out for themselves whether it is beneficial.

Of course, confronting one's problems is always harder (in the short run) than avoiding them, so therapy won't necessarily be easy or pleasant. You will need to change; so will your partner. You may have to confront parts of you that you are not satisfied with. But at the same time, you will be taking charge of your life and giving time and attention to the important things, and this can be both rewarding and satisfying.

Making the Decision to Separate

While many couples come to therapy with a desire to make their relationship better or to overcome a damaging problem, others come for help with separation. In these cases, one partner is usually more interested in separation than the other. This may be out in the open, or it may be a hidden agenda that emerges during the course of therapy. Either way, some therapy ends with the couple deciding to separate. It is highly probable that these couples would have separated anyway—but without the benefit of someone there to support them.

If you are worried that your partner has a hidden agenda behind a request to seek therapy, discuss your fears openly with him or her. If, indeed, your partner is thinking about separation, you may as well be aware of the situation. At least you can then be involved in the decision-making process.

When people contemplate separation, they are often ambivalent. But if they can be made to see that change *is* possible and that the spouse *does* care about their needs, they may reconsider and be more willing to work toward improving the relationship. Proving to your partner that you care and that you can change can sometimes make a difference. On the other hand, if things have deteriorated too far and your partner has definitely made up his or her mind, there may be no turning back.

One final word about the decision to separate: If you are thinking about this option, take your time making the decision; there is no need to hurry. Typically, relationships go downhill in small increments rather than in great bursts. So there is rarely any need to feel pressured into a decision. Think it through and try to discuss it as rationally as possible. And remember that it's quite normal to feel ambivalent. The decision you make—one way or the other—will have sweeping, long-term consequences, so think it over carefully. That way, you won't later regret having made too hasty a decision.

If you decide to separate, remember that all experiences in life, even painful ones, can provide opportunities for learning. You can use them to try to understand yourself better. Moreover, beating yourself over the head or feeling that you are worthless and inadequate is not productive. You are *not* a bad person because your relationship ended. Separation and divorce simply mean that your interaction with the other person didn't work out, but they are not a statement about you and your partner as individuals. Try not to view the situation as a personal failure. And remember that it doesn't mean that future relationships can't be different. So, replace your defeating self-talk with more coping self-instruction, and don't be so hard on yourself.

Using Negotiation to Achieve a Less Conflicted Separation

When long-term relationships end, for whatever reason, both parties often experience a wide range of emotions. While there may be a sense of relief at having ended a difficult situation, feelings of loss, pain, regret, anger, fear, sadness, and sometimes depression may also occur. Frequently, these emotions last much longer than the partners had anticipated, and their very existence may complicate the adjustment period and become a source of runaway conflict escalation, as the former partners become embroiled in continuing combat. It is common for couples to have disputes (sometimes bitter ones, lasting for months or even years) over custody of or access to the children, as well as over the settlement of financial matters. And even after these issues are resolved, there may be endless struggles for the children's loyalty. The only people these battles are likely to benefit are the former partners' respective lawyers.

Although the pain that accompanies separation usually cannot be reduced without a period of mourning for the relationship and its lost opportunities, conflict *can* be minimized. The conflict-management skills discussed in this book, even if they are used only by one person, will help keep conflict between ex-partners from escalating out of control. Searching for agreements that both parties can live with and that neither will consider unfair is likely to provide the best solution to joint problems and will allow former partners to get on with their lives without the constant irritation of unresolved conflict. If necessary, a marital therapist, court counselor, or other professional trained in mediation can help you settle on arrangements that will be satisfactory to each of you. This is much better than going through the trauma of working with lawyers (his and hers), many of whom still take a very adversarial (win-lose) approach. Of course, more and more lawyers are being trained in negotiation and mediation, so if you can find one of these, you may get the real help you need in finalizing an agreement that involves a minimum of conflict and unpleasantness. For more information on adjustment to separation and divorce, see the Further Reading section.

Marriage counseling can be helpful for couples who want to improve their relationships as well as for couples who want to end relationships. But therapy is not a panacea, and passively going along to counseling isn't likely to be effective. Marriage counseling is not something that the therapist does to you. It is something you do. It requires your active commitment to change and involvement in the change process. If both parties are willing to make this commitment, the result can be very rewarding.

However, when couples do decide to end their relationship, negotiation still provides a useful approach for arriving at mutually acceptable agreements about potentially contentious topics, such as custody of the children and division of property. A third party who can act as a mediator may be helpful, but third parties who encourage conflict should be avoided.

Finally, it is an interesting social commentary that more books are written on separation and divorce than on how to prevent it. And even books on marital therapy often end with a chapter on separation and divorce. This book, however, is more optimistic. It suggests that learning good communication, negotiation, and coupling skills can provide alternatives that will keep conflict from becoming the dominant feature in your relationship. Therefore, the last chapter in this book encourages you to meet the challenge of putting these skills to work!

22

Meeting the Challenge
of Making It Work

Managing conflict remains one of the greatest challenges facing the human race. At the international level, two world wars and countless smaller ones have wreaked havoc on millions of people during the twentieth century. The potential for another world war, with greater destruction than anything we have ever known, still poses a constant threat to our well-being.

At the intergroup level, racial, religious, and other sectarian conflicts abound. Conflict plagues most organizations at all levels, even those that are dedicated to establishing peace and justice, such as the United Nations or churches.

At the interpersonal level, the divorce rate is soaring. The incidence of child abuse is appallingly high, and assaults and homicides are on the increase.

Yet, periods of peace do exist. Countries that were bitter enemies become the best of friends. Rival groups can and do cooperate, despite their differences. Organizations persist and get the job done, regardless of their internal squabbles. People manage to form and maintain lasting and loving relationships.

As intelligent beings, we have an unprecedented choice: We can use our intelligence to try to vanquish the other side, or we can use it to resolve our differences rationally. If we attempt to prevail over the other—whoever they may be—we ultimately jeopardize our own interests and integrity, as we succumb to coercive tactics and allow conflict to escalate out of control. However, if we choose to search for solutions that allow both sides to win, we remain as committed as ever to our own objectives, but the methods for achieving them become mutual understanding and creativity.

Until recently, this choice seemed more illusory than real and such statements sounded almost utopian. But as more time and resources have been devoted to research into conflict, and as theory, data, and practical skills for managing conflict accumulate, this choice is becoming more realistic. For the first time, we *can* choose to manage conflict systematically and constructively.

Such a choice opens up a new dimension in personal responsibility. No longer are we at the mercy of our emotions or our past learning. We can achieve new heights of understanding. We can be freed from the tyranny of defending positions in which we no longer believe. We can turn, instead, to open, creative approaches to our problems that allow new solutions to emerge. We can eliminate destructive and coercive strategies, which are relationship-destroying, and replace them with relationship-enhancing strategies, without sacrificing our own interests.

The research suggests that we have been trapped in a narrow and stereotyped response to conflict. We have mistakenly assumed that resolution requires that one side wins and one side loses, and we have operated within these constraints. Unfortunately, this restricted view of the options often led us to behave in ways that we could not be proud of, and even when we did "win," the losses were often considerable, the victories hollow, not worth the sacrifice, and frequently short-lived. This erroneous way of looking at things also blinded us to the possibility of satisfactory solutions that could meet both sides' needs, resolve the conflict without adverse consequences, and preserve, instead of destroy, the relationship.

But constructive conflict management is not easy to learn. Even for the most committed practitioner, putting theory into practice can present a daunting challenge. New skills have to be learned and old habits overcome. And these new skills sometimes have to be sustained in the absence of an immediate response from the other party.

Making the choice to learn these skills and apply them—difficult though they may be—can open up a new dimension of understanding of ourselves and others. If we take up the challenge, we quickly learn that behind most conflicts is a common set of basic human needs—the need to be loved, to feel good about oneself and protect one's self-esteem, to avoid failure, to have some control over one's life, and to have one's basic requirements for living satisfied. In intimate relationships, there is an additional need that is sometimes overlooked—the need to keep the relationship intact and functioning. Since this represents an important interest in most marriages, learning how to satisfy one's partner's needs actually turns out to be in one's own self-interest.

Core needs such as the ones mentioned above are at the heart of conflict. When they are frustrated, conflicts occur. When core needs are satisfied, conflicts are less likely. It's as simple and as complicated as that.

Much of this book has been about how to understand and meet your own and your partners' needs. Like anything else worth preserving, intimate relationships require regular care. To keep your relationship working well, you will need to remember to communicate your needs, be tuned in to your partner's needs, and use negotiation skills when your needs are in conflict. You will also want to be sure to give your partner his or her fair share of love and affection. By doing this *regularly,* problems can be prevented, and when they do occur, they can be solved when they first come up, rather than ticking away like time bombs.

The strategies discussed in this book are based on the belief that behavior is governed by laws that, when understood, can be used to make relationships work better. Occasionally, couples balk at the idea that behavior—theirs or anyone else's—can be understood and managed rationally. They protest that such an approach sounds mechanical and boring and could take the magic and mystery out of relating. But this is simply not true! Regardless of how competent you become at managing conflict, you can be sure that each conflict will present new and engrossing challenges for you to master. And no matter how much time and skill you apply to trying to achieve a better understanding of your partner, he or she will always remain a different person, with a vast range of unique formative experiences and perceptions. Although, over time, you may become thoroughly familiar with your partner's habits, likes, and dislikes, the innermost region, where your partner lives, is likely to remain shrouded in mystery except for the occasional magical times when you do connect and share a brief moment of deeper understanding. Mastering the conflict-management skills presented here will, I hope, help you achieve that deeper understanding more often and allow you literally to "live more happily ever after."

Skills Review

How to Negotiate on the Basis of Interests

Conflict can be either constructive or destructive. Conflicts become destructive when they escalate out of control or they are suppressed.

This book explains how to replace positional arguing and conflict spirals with the more constructive method of negotiating on the basis of interests. Here, the goal is for both sides to have their most important needs and concerns satisfied so that both partners can win and the relationship can be preserved.

Arguments can be converted into negotiation by the following steps: (See diagram on page 246).

STEP 1: SCHEDULE A TIME TO NEGOTIATE

To set up negotiation:

- Schedule regular sessions (e.g., weekly)
- Add special, ad hoc sessions when necessary
- Choose times when you are not angry, won't be interrupted, and have not been overdrinking

When it's time to negotiate:

- Sit down side by side (rather than across from each other)
- Define the issue to be negotiated—focus on the future, not the past
- Set a time limit and continue at another time if you don't finish

STEP 2: EXPLORE YOUR PARTNER'S INTERESTS (NEEDS AND WANTS, FEARS AND CONCERNS)

Ask your partner:

- What do you want/need from this situation?
- Is there anything that concerns or worries you about this situation?
- Do you have any other interests . . . ?

If your partner has already taken a position, ask:

- What needs or concerns would your position satisfy?
- What worries or concerns do you have about doing something else?

Probe further to discover deeper issues. Remember, the most important interests are basic human needs, such as:

- The need to be loved
- The need for acceptance and recognition
- The need to avoid failure
- The need to feel in control

As your partner speaks:

- Look at your partner and listen carefully
- Give encouragement (e.g., nod and say "uh-huh," "I see," etc.)
- Don't interrupt
- Ask clarifying questions
- Listen for meaning
- Probe for deeper interests
- Reflect what you have heard
- Write down your partner's interests
- Don't criticize, evaluate, guess, or try to mind read
- Summarize and ask if your summary is correct
- If it isn't, ask for clarification and resummarize
- Ask your partner to identify his or her most important interests and circle them

STEP 3: EXPLAIN YOUR OWN INTERESTS

Ask:

- What do I want from this situation?
- What are my needs in this situation?
- Is there anything that worries or concerns me?

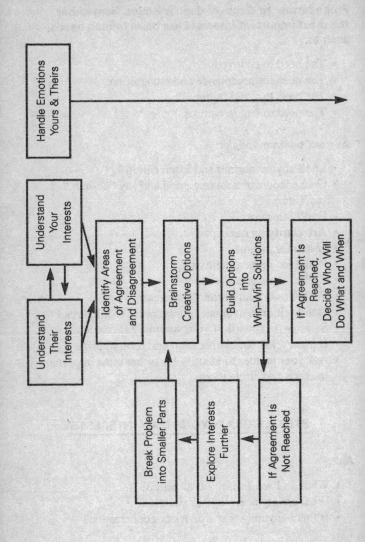

If you have already taken a position, try to discover what interests lie behind it. Ask:

- Why do I want that solution?
- What needs or wants would that solution satisfy?
- What worries or concerns would I have about doing something else?

When you explore interests:

- State your interests clearly
- *Don't* discuss your "position"
- Resist urges to make provocative comments
- Try to explore the deeper issues
- Ask your partner to record your interests
- Identify the most important ones and circle them
- Ask your partner to summarize
- Provide clarification if necessary and have your partner resummarize until a full understanding is achieved

STEP 4: BRAINSTORM CREATIVE OPTIONS BASED ON BOTH PARTIES' INTERESTS

- Draw a line between common interests to identify those you have in common and those that are different

With the list of both parties' interests in front of you:

- Be as creative as possible
- Don't evaluate or criticize
- Don't censor any ideas (including your own)
- If necessary, remind your partner of the no-criticizing rule
- Write down all ideas

- Keep going until you run out of ideas and have a long list
- Review the list and circle the most promising ideas

STEP 5: BUILD CREATIVE OPTIONS INTO WIN-WIN SOLUTIONS

To build win-win solutions:

- Piece together promising options to meet each party's most important interests
- Write these down
- Be honest if you don't like a solution
- Try different combinations until you have several solutions
- Choose the best solution and develop it further
- Ask, What would make it better?
- Ask, Are we happy with this solution? Do we both consider it fair? Will it resolve our problem?

If a win-win solution is not found:

- Take a break and try again later
- Reexplore interests to see if there are any hidden agendas
- Do some additional brainstorming
- Consider dividing the problem into smaller sections
- Consider expanding the area to be negotiated

Once a win-win solution is found:

- Plan who will do what by when
- Write down the plan
- Schedule a time to discuss progress

- Do what you have agreed to do regardless of your partner's response
- If your partner doesn't follow through, express your disappointment

STEP 6: MANAGE YOUR EMOTIONS

To prevent angry feelings:

- Consider alternative interpretations of events
- Try to see things from your partner's perspective
- Don't review angry thoughts
- Use calming self-talk (e.g., "Relax," "Just stay calm," etc.)
- Act calm—talk slowly and don't raise your voice
- Relax by taking a few deep breaths, relaxing tense muscles, imagining yourself in a relaxing setting

If you do become emotional:

- Say how you feel and why (e.g., "I'm feeling upset because . . .")
- Replace angry self-talk with calming self-talk
- Resist the urge to attack your partner—don't accuse, insult, or call names
- Use less-dogmatic phrases (e.g., "It seems . . ." or "I think . . .")
- Say you want to take time out and reschedule the negotiation session
- Let go of your anger with exercise, relaxation, music, or humor
- Return to a problem-solving mode
- Praise yourself if you succeed in handling your emotions
- Seek professional help if anger is a serious problem

STEP 7: HANDLE YOUR PARTNER'S EMOTIONS

When your partner becomes angry:

- Let your partner talk
- Listen
- Ask questions to clarify feelings and your partner's view of the situation
- Acknowledge the other's feelings and summarize your understanding ("It sounds as though you are feeling———because of ———. Is that right?")
- Don't respond to personal attacks, and resist the urge to defend yourself
- Address feelings of hurt and let your partner know that you are sorry that he or she is upset
- Use calming self-talk to keep cool
- Refuse to argue but be willing to negotiate
- Return to the negotiation process (e.g., "Let's get back to discussing your interests")

ADVANCED STAGES: USE THE TYPE OF NEGOTIATION THAT FITS THE SITUATION

***Meta-negotiation,* which involves negotiating over the negotiation process, is useful when:**

- The process escalates out of control
- The parties have concerns about negotiating
- A hidden agenda is present and the wrong issue is being addressed

Comprehensive negotiation is useful when:

- Relationship rules are needed to allocate privileges, responsibilities, and decision making

- There is disagreement over an important issue
- An issue causes repeated conflict
- Roles need to be renegotiated due to changing circumstances

Brief negotiation is useful when:

- The issue is of minor importance
- The issue can be resolved quickly with a few creative suggestions

Adopt a principle of reciprocity over time and across situations as your standard of fairness.

HOW TO THINK MORE CONSTRUCTIVELY ABOUT YOUR RELATIONSHIP

How you think about your partner and your relationship *can* affect how you feel.

To prevent unnecessary conflict:

- Be careful not to dwell on your partner's "faults"
- Focus on your partner's more positive qualities
- Consider whether you might be contributing to your partner's behavior
- Refrain from assuming the worst
- Give your partner the benefit of the doubt
- Consider alternative hypotheses
- Don't try to mind read—instead, ask
- Try to see things from your partner's perspective
- Don't dismiss your partner's nice gestures as insincere—enjoy them!
- Question your expectations about what "should" and "shouldn't" be

- Accept that everything won't always be the way you would like it to be
- Try to be more accepting of your own and your partner's behavior
- Give up unrealistic fantasies about ideal relationships
- Change pessimistic thoughts to more optimistic ones

HOW TO ASK FOR WHAT YOU WANT

Unnecessary conflict can be prevented when partners meet each other's needs. But don't expect your partner to be able to mind read. Tell him or her what you want by making a simple request.

To make a simple request:

- Say, "I'd like . . ." or "I want . . ." followed by the request
- Make your request specific rather than vague
- Make it positive rather than negative
- Negotiate, if your request conflicts with your partner's interests

Change complaints into requests for change.

To make a request for change:

- Use "I statements" in place of "you statements"
- Say, "I feel————when you————. In the future I'd like it if you would————."
- Be specific about what you want in the future
- Don't discuss the past

- Repeat requests if they are ignored
- Negotiate if your partner doesn't agree to the request for change

Listen to your partner's requests for change and respond by:

- Agreeing if you can make the change without sacrificing your interests
- Saying "no" and negotiating if the request conflicts with your interests

Learning to make simple requests and requests for change can overcome mind reading and cross-complaining and lead to more honest communication and better understanding.

HOW TO REINTRODUCE LOVING BEHAVIORS INTO YOUR RELATIONSHIP

Reintroducing loving behaviors can increase your positive feelings for each other and lower your threshold for conflict.

Look for coupling activities that you can do together. For example:

- Plan a night out on the town
- Learn to do something new
- Take up something you've enjoyed in the past
- Think up simple activities
- Make new friends
- Get away for a vacation or a weekend

Increase your physical affection by:

- Touching
- Kissing
- Hugging
- Stroking
- Caressing
- Cuddling
- Holding
- Asking for affection when you need it (e.g., "Can I have a hug?")

Give your partner more verbal affection:

- Tell your partner that you care
- Use endearing names
- Praise your partner's physical features
- Acknowledge efforts to look attractive
- Express your appreciation for behaviors that you like
- Admire some aspect of your partner's personality
- Tell your partner that he or she is wonderful

Think up creative romantic gestures and carry them out:

- Plan a special outing or event
- Give your partner a romantic gift
- Pamper your partner in a special way
- Plan a surprise

Work on making sex better by:

- Talking about how it could be improved
- Saying what *you* want as clearly as possible
- Making an effort to overcome your inhibitions
- Spending some time and effort to get the mood right
- Trying out your partner's suggestions/directions

- Asking for feedback
- Being more creative
- Using the negotiation method to resolve conflicts about sex
- Reading the recommended books
- Getting professional help for serious sexual problems

To increase the loving behaviors in your relationship, consider:

- Doing a *minimum* of five caring behaviors every day
- Planning "caring days" for each other

So, show your partner that you care, listen, try to understand his or her perspective, be clear about expressing your own needs, and when your needs are in conflict, negotiate.

Further Reading

Alcohol Problems

Miller, W.R., and R.F. Munoz. 1976. *How to Control Your Drinking*. Englewood Cliffs, New Jersey: Prentice Hall.

Anger

Hankins, Gary. *Prescription for Anger: Coping with Angry Feelings and Angry People*. New York: Warner Books.

Novaco, R.W. 1975. *Anger Control*. Lexington, Massachusetts: D.C. Heath and Co.

Assertive Training

Alberti, R.E., and M.L. Emmons. 1971. *Your Perfect Right*. San Luis Obispo, California: Impact.

Fensterheim, H., and J. Baer. 1976. *Don't Say Yes When You Want to Say No*. London: Dell Publications.

Jaberbowski, P., and A.J. Lange. 1978. *The Assertive Option: Your Rights and Responsibilities*. Champaign, Illinois: Research Press.

Shaw, M.E., E. Wallace, and F.N. Labella. 1980. *Making It Assertively*. Englewood Cliffs, New Jersey: Prentice Hall.

Smith, M.J. 1975. *When I Say No I Feel Guilty*. New York: Dial Press.

Change

Calhoun, L.G., J.W. Selby, and E. King. 1977. *Dealing with Crises: A Guide to Critical Life Problems*. Englewood Cliffs, New Jersey: Prentice Hall.

Dyer, W.W. 1977. *Your Erroneous Zones*. London: Sphere.

Egan, G. 1977. *You and Me: The Skills of Communicating and Relating to Others*. Monterey, California: Brooks/Cole.

Ellis, A. and R.A. Harper. 1975. *A New Guide to Rational Living*. Englewood Cliffs, New Jersey: Prentice Hall.

Freeman, L. 1978. *The Sorrow and the Fury: Overcoming Hurt and Loss from Childhood to Old Age*. Englewood Cliffs, New Jersey: Prentice Hall.

Goldstein, A.P., R.P. Sprafhim, and N.J. Gershaw. 1979. *I Know What's Wrong But I Don't Know What To Do About It*. Englewood Cliffs, New Jersey: Prentice Hall.

Mahoney, M.J. 1979. *Self-change Strategies for Solving Personal Problems*. New York: Norton.

Newman, M., and B. Berkowitz. 1978. *How to Take Charge of Your Life*. London: Bantam Books.

Zastrow, C., and D. H. Chang, eds. 1977. *The Personal Problem Solver*. Englewood Cliffs, New Jersey: Prentice Hall.

Zastrow, C. 1979. *Talk to Yourself: Using the Power of Self Talk*. Englewood Cliffs, New Jersey: Prentice Hall.

Depression

Lewisohn, P., R. Munoz, A. Zeiss, and M.A. Youngren. 1979. *Control Your Depression*. Englewood Cliffs, New Jersey: Prentice Hall.

Rush, J. 1983. *Beating Depression*. London: Century.

Divorce

Adam, J., and N. Adam. 1979. *Divorce: How and When to Let Go*. Englewood Cliffs, New Jersey: Prentice Hall.

Krantler, M. 1974. *Creative Divorce*. New York: New American Library.

Wheeler, M. 1975. *No Fault Divorce*. Boston: Beacon Press.

Fears

Marks, I.M. 1978. *Living with Fears: Understanding and Coping with Anxiety*. New York: McGraw-Hill.

Rosen, G. 1977. *Don't Be Afraid: A Program for Overcoming Fears and Phobias*. Englewood Cliffs, New Jersey: Prentice Hall.

Children

Gordan, T. 1970. *Parent Effectiveness Training*. New York: Wyden.

Patterson, G.R. 1978. *Families*. Champaign, Illinois: Research Press.

Rubin, J. and C. Rubin. 1989. *When Families Fight*. New York: Arbor House/William Morrow & Co.

Leisure

Lowen, A. 1976. *Pleasure: A Creative Approach to Life*. London: Penguin.

Rapoport, R., and R.N. Rapoport. 1978. *Leisure and the Family Life*. London: Routledge and Kegan Paul.

Marital

Bach, G.R., and P. Wyden. 1968. *The Intimate Enemy*. New York: Avon.

Gottman, J., C. Notarius, J. Gonso, and H. Markman. 1976. *A Couple's Guide to Communication*. Champaign, Illinois: Research Press.

Montgomery, B. and L. Evans. 1983. *Living and Loving Together*. Melbourne, Australia: Nelson.

Zwell, M. 1978. *How to Succeed at Love*. Englewood Cliffs, New Jersey: Prentice Hall.

Negotiation

Fisher, R., and S. Brown. 1988. *Getting Together: Building a Relationship That Gets to Yes*. Boston: Houghton Mifflin.

Fisher, R., and W. Ury. 1981. *Getting to Yes*. London: Hutchinson.

Relaxation and Stress

Rosen, G. 1978. *The Relaxation Book: An Illustrated Self-help Program*. Englewood Cliffs, New Jersey: Prentice Hall.

Selye, H. 1977. *Stress Without Disaster: How to Survive in a Stressful Society*. Sevenoaks, England: Teach Yourself Books.

Sexual Issues

Comfort, A. 1972. *The Joy of Sex*. London: Quartet Books.
————— 1973. *More Joy of Sex*. London: Quartet Books.
Gochros, H.L., and J. Fischer. 1980. *Treat Yourself to a Better Sex Life*. Englewood Cliffs, New Jersey: Prentice Hall.
Heiman, J., L. LoPiccolo, and J. LoPiccolo. 1976. *Becoming Orgasmic: A Sexual Growth Program for Woman*. Englewood Cliffs, New Jersey: Prentice Hall.
Hite, S. 1976. *The Hite Report*. London: Corgi.
—————. 1981. *The Hite Report on Male Sexuality*. London: MacDonald.

Women's Issues

Friedman, S., L. Gams, N. Gottlieb, and C. Nesselson. 1979. *A Woman's Guide to Therapy*. Englewood Cliffs, New Jersey: Prentice Hall.
Orbach, S., and L. Eichenbaum. 1984. *What Do Women Want?* London: Fontana.

Work Issues

Cooper, G.L., and R. Payne. 1978. *Stress at Work*. Chichester: Wiley and Sons.
Levene, M. 1976. *The Second Time Around: Second Careers and How to Make Then More Successful Than the First*. London: Davis-Poyner.

References

Alschuler, C.F., and A.S. Alschuler. 1984. Developing healthy responses to anger: The counselor's role. *Journal of Counseling and Development* 63, 26–29.

Azrin, N., B.J. Master, and R. Jones. 1973. Reciprocity counseling: A rapid learning-based procedure for marital counseling. *Behavior Research and Therapy* 11, 365–82.

Barry, W.A. 1970. Marriage research and conflict: An integrative review. *Psychological Bulletin* 73, 41–54.

Barsky, M. 1983. Emotional needs and dysfunctional communication as blocks to mediation. *Mediation Quarterly* 2, 55–66.

Baruth, L.G., and C.H. Huber. 1984. *An Introduction to Marital Theory and Therapy.* Monterey, California: Brooks/Cole.

Baucom, D.H. 1982. A comparison of behavioral contracting and problem solving/communications training in behavioral marital therapy. *Behavior Therapy* 13, 161–74.

Baucom, D.H., and P.A. Aiken. 1984. Sex role identity, marital satisfaction, and response to behavioral marital therapy. *Journal of Consulting and Clinical Psychology* 52, 438–44.

Bausom, D.H., and G.W. Lester. 1986. The usefulness of cognitive restructuring as an adjunct to behavioral marital therapy. *Behavior Therapy* 17, 385–403.

Bennun, I. 1986. Cognitive components in marital conflict. *Behavioural Psychotherapy* 14, 302–09.

———. 1987. Behavioural marital therapy: A critique and appraisal of integrated models. *Behavioural Psychotherapy* 15, 1–15.

Bentler, P.M., and M.D. Newcomb. 1978. Longitudinal study of marital success and failure. *Journal of Consulting and Clinical Psychology* 46, 1053–70.

Birchler, G.R. 1979. Communication skills in married couples. In A.S. Bellack and M. Hersen eds. *Research and Practice in Social Skills Training*. New York: Plenum Press.

Birchler, G.R., and L.J. Webb. 1977. Discriminating interaction behaviors in happy and unhappy marriages. *Journal of Consulting and Clinical Psychology* 45, 494–95.

Bloom, B.L., S.J. Asher, and S.W. White. 1978. Marital disruption as a stressor: A review and analysis. *Psychological Bulletin* 85, 867–94.

Bornstein, P.H., J.S. Hickey, M.J. Schulein, S.G. Fox, and M.J. Scolatti. 1983. Behavioural-communications treatment of marital interaction: Negative behaviours. *British Journal of Clinical Psychology* 22, 41–48.

Brockner, J., and J.Z. Rubin. 1985. *Entrapment in Escalating Conflicts: A Social Psychological Analysis*. New York: Springer-Verlag.

Burton, J. 1969. *Conflict and Communication*. New York: Macmillan.

Bussod, N., and N.S. Jacobson. 1983. Cognitive behavioral marital therapy. *Counselling Psychologist* 11, 57–63.

Conoley, C.W., J.C. Conoley, J.A. McConnell, and C.E. Kimzey. 1983. The effects of the ABCs of Rational Emotive Therapy and the Empty Chair Technique of Gestalt Therapy on anger reduction. *Psychotherapy: Theory, Research and Practice* 20, 112–17.

Deutsch, M. 1973. *The Resolution of Conflict: Constructive Versus Destructive Processes*. New Haven, Connecticut: Yale University Press.

———. 1975. Equity, equality, and need: What determines which values will be used as a basis of distributive justice? *Journal of Social Issues* 31, 137–1149.

Doherty, W.J. 1982. Attributional style and negative problem solving in marriage. *Family Relationships* 31, 201–05.

Druckman, D. ed. 1977. *Negotiations: Social-psychological Perspectives*. Beverly Hills, California: Sage Publications.

Eidelsen, R.J., and N. Epstein. 1982. Cognition and relationship maladjustment: Development of a measure of dysfunctional relationship beliefs. *Journal of Consulting and Clinical Psychology* 50, 715–20.

Ellis, A. 1976. Techniques of handling anger in marriage. *Journal of Marriage and Family Counseling* 2, 305–15.

———. 1977. *Anger: How to Live with and Without It*. Secaucus, New Jersey: Citadel Press.

———. 1985. Love and its problems. In A. Ellis and M.E. Bernard, eds. *Clinical Applications of Rational Emotive Therapy*. New York: Plenum Press.

———. 1986. Rational-emotive therapy applied to relationship therapy. *Journal of Rational Emotive Therapy* 4, 4–21.

Emery, R.E. 1982. Interparental conflict and the children of discord and divorce. *Psychological Bulletin* 92, 310–30.

Epstein, N. 1982. Cognitive therapy with couples. *The American Journal of Family Therapy* 10, 5–15.

Filley, A.C. 1975. *Interpersonal Conflict Resolution*. Glenview, Illinois: Scott, Foresman and Co.

Filsinger, E.E., and R.A. Lewis, eds. 1981. *Assessing Marriage: New Behavioral Approaches*. Beverly Hills, California: Sage Publications.

Fincham, F.D. 1985. Attribution processes in distressed and nondistressed couples: 2. Responsibility for marital problems. *Journal of Abnormal Psychology* 2, 183–90.

Fincham, F.D., and T.N. Bradbury. 1987. Cognitive processes and conflict in close relationships: An attribution-efficacy model. *Journal of Personality and Social Psychology* 53, 1106–18.

Fincham, F., and K.D. O'Leary. 1983. Causal inferences for spouse behavior in maritally distressed and nondistressed couples. *Journal of Social and Clinical Psychology* 1, 42–57.

Fisher, R. 1964. Fractionating conflict. In R. Fisher, ed. *International Conflict and Behavioral Science*. New York: Basic Books.

———. 1986. The structure of negotiation: An alternative model. *Negotiation Journal* 2, 233–36.

Fisher, R., and S. Brown. 1988. *Getting Together: Building a Relationship That Gets to Yes*. Boston: Houghton Mifflin.

Fisher, R., and W.H. Davis. 1987. Six basic interpersonal skills for a negotiator's repertoire. *Negotiation Journal* 3, 117–22.

Fisher, R., and W. Ury. 1981. *Getting to Yes*. London: Hutchinson.

Fishman, C.A., and A.S. Alschuler. 1984. Developing healthy responses to anger: The counselor's role. *Journal of Counseling and Development* 63, 26–29.

Frederickson, C.G. 1977. Life stress and marital conflict: A pilot study. *Journal of Marriage and Family Counseling* 3, 41–47.

Gelles, R.J. 1974. *The Violent Home: A Study of Physical Aggression between Husbands and Wives*. New York: Sage Publications.

Gillespie, D.L. 1971. Who has the power? The marital struggle. *Journal of Marriage and the Family* 33, 445–58.

Glenn, N.W., and C.N. Weaver. 1977. The marital happiness of remarried divorced persons. *Journal of Marriage and the Family* 39, 331–37.

———. 1978. A multivariate, multisurvey of marital happiness. *Journal of Marriage and the Family* 40, 269–82.

Glick, P.C., and S. Lin. 1986. Recent changes in divorce and remarriage. *Journal of Marriage and the Family* 48, 437–747.

Goldberg, S.B., E.D. Green, and F.E. Sander. 1987. Saying you're sorry. *Negotiation Journal* 3, 221–24.

Gottman, J. 1979. *Marital Interaction: Experimental Investigations*. New York: Academic Press.

Gottman, J., C. Notarius, J. Gonso, and H. Markman. 1976. *A Couple's Guide to Communication*. Champaign, Illinois: Research Press.

Gottman, J., C. Notarius, H. Markman, S. Bank, B. Yoppi, and M.E. Rubin. 1976. Behavior exchange theory and marital decision making. *Journal of Personality and Social Psychology* 34, 14–23.

Gottman, J., H. Markman, and C. Notarius. 1977. The topography of marital conflict: A sequential analysis of verbal and nonverbal behavior. *Journal of Marriage and the Family* 39, 461–77.

Greenbaum, M. 1986. Resolving conflict—without conflicts of interest. *Negotiation Journal* 2, 121–28.

Greene, G.J., and P. Kelley. 1985. Cognitive relationship enhancement: An exploratory study. *Family Therapy* 12, 231–44.

Greenhalgh, L. 1987. The case against winning in negotiation. *Negotiation Journal* 3, 167–73.

———. 1987. Relationships in negotiations. *Negotiation Journal* 3, 235–44.

Gurman, A.S., and D.P. Kniskern. Research on marital and family therapy: Progress, perspective and prospect. In S.L. Garfield and A.E. Bergin, eds. *Handbook of Psychotherapy and Behavior Change: An Empirical Analysis*. New York: Wiley.

Hahlweg, K., and N.S. Jacobson, eds. 1984. *Marital Interaction: Analysis and Modification*. New York: Guilford Press.

Hahlweg, K., D. Revenstorf, and L. Schindler. 1984. Effects of behavioral marital therapy on couples' communication and problem-solving skills. *Journal of Consulting and Clinical Psychology* 52, 553–66.

Halford, K., and M. Sanders. 1985. Behavioural marital therapy: Current status, limitations, and directions for further research. *Behaviour Change* 2, 36–42.

Hankins, G., and C. Hankins. 1993. *Prescription for Anger*. New York: Warner Books.

Harrell, J., and B. Guerney. 1976. Training married couples in conflict negotiation skills. In D.H.L. Olson, ed. *Treating Relationships*. Lake Mills, Iowa: Graphic Publishing Co.

Havemann, E., and M. Lehtinen. 1986. *Marriages and Families: New Problems, New Opportunities*. Englewood Cliffs, New Jersey: Prentice Hall.

Haynes, J.M. 1988. Working with families when spousal and parenting roles are confused. *Negotiation Journal* 4, 171–82.

Hazaleus, S.L., and J.L. Deffenbacher. 1986. Relaxation and cognitive treatments of anger. *Journal of Consulting and Clinical Psychology* 54, 222–26.

Hickok, J.E., and M.G. Komechak. 1974. Behavior modification in marital conflict: A case report. *Family Process* 13, 111–19.

Hotaling, T.G. 1980. Attribution processes in husband-wife violence. In M.A. Strauss and G.T. Hotaling, eds. *The So-

cial Causes of Husband-Wife Violence. Minnesota: University of Minnesota Press.

Howe, G.W. 1987. Attributions of complex cause and the perception of marital conflict. *Journal of Personality and Social Psychology* 53, 1119–28.

Huber, C.H., and B. Milstein. 1985. Cognitive restructuring and a collaborative set in couples' work. *The American Journal of Family Therapy* 13, 17–27.

Hunt, M., and B. Hunt. 1978. *Divorce Experience: A New Look at the World of the Formerly Married*. New York: McGraw-Hill.

Katz, N., and S. Thorson. 1988. Theory and practice: A pernicious separation? *Negotiation Journal* 4, 115–18.

King, K.N. 1988. But I'm not a funny person—Humor in dispute resolution. *Negotiation Journal* 2, 119–23.

Kolb, T.M., and M.A. Straus. 1974. Marital power and marital happiness in relation to problem solving. *Journal of Marriage and the Family* 36, 756–866.

Jacobson, N.S. 1977. Training couples to solve their marital problems: A behavioral approach to relationship discord. *International Journal of Family Counseling* 4, 22–31.

———. 1977. Problem solving and contingency contracting in the treatment of marital discord. *Journal of Consulting and Clinical Psychology* 45, 92–100.

———1978. A stimulus control model of change in behavioral couples' therapy: Implications for contingency contracting. *Journal of Marriage and Family Counseling* 4, 35–39.

———. 1978. Specific and nonspecific factors in the effectiveness of a behavioral approach to the treatment of marital discord. *Journal of Consulting and Clinical Psychology* 46, 442–52.

———. 1979. Behavioral treatments for marital discord. A critical approach. In M. Hersen, R.M. Eisler, and P.M.

Miller, eds. *Progress in Behavior Modification*. New York: Academic Press.

————. 1984. A component analysis of behavioral marital therapy: The relative effectiveness of behavior exchange and communication/problem solving training. *Journal of Consulting and Clinical Psychology* 52, 294–305.

Jacobson, N.S., W.C. Follette, D. Revenstorf, K. Hahlweg, O.H. Baucom, and G. Margolin. 1984. Variability in outcome and clinical significance of behavioral marital therapy: A reanalysis of outcome data. *Journal of Consulting and Clinical Psychology* 52, 497–504.

Jacobson, N.S., V.M. Follette, W.C. Follette, A. Holtzworth-Munroe, J.L. Katt, and K.B. Schmaling. 1985. A component analysis of behavioral marital therapy: One year follow-up. *Behavior Research and Therapy* 23, 549–55.

Jacobson, N.S., and A.S. Gurman, eds. *Clinical Handbook of Marital Therapy*. New York: Guilford Press.

Jacobson, N.S., and G. Margolin. 1979. Marital Therapy: Strategies Based on Social Learning and Behavior Exchange Principles. *New York: Bruner/Mazel*.

Jacobson, N.S., and B. Martin. 1976. Behavioral marriage therapy: Current status. *Psychological Bulletin* 83, 540–56.

Jacobson, N.S., D.W. McDonald, W.C. Follette, and R.A. Berley. 1985. Attribution processes in distressed and nondistressed married couples. *Cognitive Therapy and Research* 9, 35–50.

Jacobson, N.S., H. Waldron, and D. Moore. 1980. Toward a behavioral profile of marital distress. *Journal of Consulting and Clinical Psychology* 49, 269–77.

Johnson, S.M., and L.S. Greenberg. 1985. Differential effects of experiential and problem-solving interventions in resolving marital conflict. *Journal of Consulting and Clinical Psychology* 53, 175—84.

Kelley, H., E. Berscheid, A. Christensen, J.H. Harvey, T.L.

Huston, G. Levinger, E. McClintock, L.A. Peplau, and D.R. Peterson. 1983. *Close Relationships*. New York: Freeman.

Kressel, K.K. 1985. *The Process of Divorce: How Professionals and Couples Negotiate Settlements*. New York: Basic Books.

Kriesberg, L. 1987. Timing and the initiation of de-escalation moves. *Negotiation Journal* 3, 375–84.

Lange, A.J., and P. Jakubowski. 1976. *Responsible Assertive Behavior*. Champaign, Illinois: Research Press.

Lax, D.A., and J.K. Sebenius. 1986. Interests: The measure of negotiation. *Negotiation Journal* 2, 73–92.

Lenthall, G. 1977. Marital satisfaction and marital stability. *Journal of Marriage and Family Counseling* 3, 25–31.

Lewicki, R.J., and J.A. Litterer. 1985. *Negotiation,* vol. 1. Homewood, Illinois: Irwin.

Levinger, G. 1976. A social psychological perspective on marital dissolution. *Journal of Social Issues* 32, 21–47.

Liberman, R.P. 1970. Behavioral approaches to family and couple therapy. *American Journal of Orthopsychiatry* 40, 106–18.

Liberman, R.P., E. Wheeler, and N. Sanders. 1976. Behavioral therapy for marital disharmony: An educational approach. *Journal of Marriage and Family Counseling* 2, 383–95..

Liberman, R.P., E.G. Wheeler, L.A. DeVisser, J. Kuehnel, and T. Kuehnel. 1979. *Handbook of Marital Therapy*. New York: Plenum.

Little, M. 1982. *Family Breakup: Understanding Marital Problems and the Mediating of Child Custody Decisions*. San Francisco: Jossey-Bass.

Lindskold, S. 1978. Trust development, the GRIT proposal, and the effects of conciliatory acts on conflict and cooperation. *Psychological Bulletin* 85, 772–93.

Lindskold, S., and M.L. Finch. 1981. Styles of announcing conciliation. *Journal of Conflict Resolution* 25, 145–55.

Lindskold, S., and P.S. Walters. 1986. Transforming competitive or cooperative climates. *Journal of Conflict Resolution* 30, 99–115.

Mace, D.R. 1976. Marital intimacy and the deadly love-anger cycle. *Journal of Marriage and Family Counseling* 2, 131–37.

Madden, M.E., and R. Janoff-Bulman. 1981. Blame, control and marital satisfaction: Wives' attributions for conflict in marriage. *Journal of Marriage and the Family* 44, 663–74.

Margolin, G.A. 1978. A multilevel approach to the assessment of communication positiveness in distressed couples. International *Journal of Family Counseling* 6, 81–89.

———. 1979. Conjoint marital therapy to enhance anger management and reduce spouse abuse. *American Journal of Family Therapy* 2, 12–23.

———. 1981. A behavioral systems approach to the treatment of marital jealousy. *Clinical Psychology Review* 1, 479–87.

Margolin, G., V. Fernandez, S. Talovic, and R. Onorato. 1983. Sex role considerations and behavioral marital therapy: Equal does not mean identical. *Journal of Marital and Family Therapy* 9, 131–45.

Margolin, G. and B.E. Wampold. 1981. Sequential analysis of conflict and accord in distressed and nondistressed marital partners. *Journal of Consulting and Clinical Psychology* 49, 554–67.

Margolin, G., and R.L. Weiss. 1978. Communication training and assessment: A case of behavioral marital enrichment. *Behavior Therapy* 9, 508–20.

Miller, P.C., H.M. Lefcourt, J.G. Holmes, E.E. Ware, and W.E. Saleh. 1986. Marital locus of control and marital problem solving. *Journal of Personality and Social Psychology* 51, 161–69.

Miller S., E.W. Nunnally, and D.B. Wackman. 1975. *Alive and Aware: Improving Communication in Relationships*. Minneapolis: Interpersonal Communications Programs.

Miller, S., E.W. Nunnally, D.B. Wackman, and R.H. Ferris. 1976. *Couple Workbook: Increasing Awareness and Communication Skills*. Minneapolis: Interpersonal Communication Programs.

Moon, J.R., and R.M. Eisler. 1983. Anger control: An experimental comparison of three behavioral treatments. *Behavior Therapy* 14, 493–505.

Murray, J.S. 1986. Understanding competing theories of negotiation. *Negotiation Journal* 2, 179–86.

Murphy, K.C. A cognitive-behavioral approach to client anxiety, anger, depression and guilt. *The Personnel and Guidance Journal* 59, 202–05.

Neidig, P.H., D.H. Friedman, and B.S. Collins. 1985. Domestic conflict containment: A spouse abuse treatment program. Social Casework: *The Journal of Contemporary Social Work*, April, 195–204.

Norton, A.J., and P.C. Glick. 1976. Marital instability: Past, present and future. *Journal of Social Issues* 32, 5–20.

Novaco, R.W. 1975. *Anger Control*. Lexington, Massachusetts: D.C. Heath and Co.

———. 1976. The functions and regulation of the arousal of anger. American *Journal of Psychiatry* 133, 1124–28.

———. 1976. Treatment of chronic anger through cognitive and relaxation controls. *Journal of Consulting and Clinical Psychology* 44, 681.

Nye, F.I., and S. McLaughlin. 1976. Role competence and marital satisfaction. In F.I. Nye, ed. *Role Structure and Analysis of the Family*. Beverly Hills, California: Sage Publications.

O'Leary, K.D., and H. Turkewitz. 1981. A comparative outcome study of behavioral marital therapy and communication therapy. *Journal of Marital and Family Therapy* 7,
   159–69.

Orvis, B.R., H.H. Kelley, and D. Butler. 1976. Attributional
   conflict in young couples. In J.H. Harvey, W. Ickes, and R.
   Kidd, eds. *New Directions in Attributional Research*, vol.
   2. Hillsdale, New Jersey: Erlbaum.

Osgood, C.E. 1962. *An Alternative to War or Surrender.* Ur-
   bana, Illinois: University of Illinois Press.

Paolino, T.J., and B.S. McCrady. 1977. *The Alcoholic Marriage: Alternative Perspectives.* New York: Grune & Strat-
   ton, Inc.

Patterson, G.R., and H. Hops. 1972. Coercion, a game for
   two: Intervention techniques for marital conflict. In R.E.
   Ulrich and P. Montjoy, eds. *The Experimental Analysis of
   Social Behavior.* New York: Appleton-Century-Crofts.

Patterson, G.R., H. Hops, and R. Weiss. 1975. Interpersonal
   skills training for couples in early stages of conflict. *Journal of Marriage and Family Counseling* 37, 295–303.

Patterson, G. R., and J.B. Reid. 1976. Reciprocity and coercion: Two facets of social systems. In C. Neuringer and J.
   Michael, eds. *Behavior Modification in Clinical Psychology.* New York: Appleton-Century-Crofts.

Patterson, G.R., R.L. Weiss, and H. Hops. 1976. Training of
   marital skills: Some problems and concepts. In H. Leiten-
   berg, ed. *Handbook of Behavior Modification.* New York:
   Appleton-Century-Crofts.

Peterson, G.R., L.W. Frederiksen, and M.S. Rosenbaum.
   1981. Developing behavioral competencies in distressed
   marital couples. *The American Journal of Family Therapy*
   9, 13–23.

Piercy, F.P. 1983. A game for interrupting coercive marital interactions. *Journal of Marital and Family Therapy* 9, 435–36.

Pruitt, D.G. 1981. *Negotiation Behavior*. New York: Academic Press.

———. 1986. Trends in the scientific study of negotiation and mediation. *Negotiation Journal* 2, 237–44.

Pruitt, D.G., and J.Z. Rubin. 1986. *Social Conflict: Escalation, Stalemate and Settlement*. New York: Random House.

Rahaim, S., C. Lefebvre, and J.O. Jenkins. 1980. The effects of social skills training on behavioral and cognitive components of anger management. *Journal of Behavior Therapy and Experimental Psychiatry* 11, 3–8.

Raiffa, H. 1982. *The Art and Science of Negotiation*. Cambridge, Massachusetts: Harvard University Press.

Rappaport, A.J., and J.A. Harrell. 1972. A behavioral-exchange model for marital counseling. *The Family Coordinator* 21, 203–12.

Renne, K.S. 1970. Correlates of dissatisfaction in marriage. *Journal of Marriage and the Family* 32, 54–67.

Rollins, B.C., and K.L. Cannon. 1974. Marital satisfaction over the family life cycle: A re-evaluation. *Journal of Marriage and the Family* 36, 271–83.

Rubin, J.Z., and B.R. Brown. 1975. *The Social Psychology of Bargaining and Negotiation*. New York: Academic Press.

Rubin, J., and C. Rubin. 1989. *When Families Fight*. New York: Arbor House/William Morrow and Co.

Sherif, M., O.J. Harvey, B.J. White, W.R. Hood, and C.W. Sherif. 1961. *Intergroup Cooperation and Competition: The Robbers Cave Experiment*. Norman, Oklahoma; University Book Exchange.

Smoke, R. 1986. The nature and control of escalation. In R. White, ed. *Psychology and the Prevention of Nuclear War*. New York: New York University Press.

Strong, J.R. 1975. A marital conflict resolution model: Redefining conflict to achieve intimacy. *Journal of Marriage and Family Counseling* 1, 269–76.

Stuart, R.B. 1969. Operant-interpersonal treatment for marital discord. *Journal of Consulting and Clinical Psychology* 33, 675–82.

———. 1980. *Helping Couples Change*. New York: Guilford Press.

Stuart, R.B., and B. Jacobson. 1985. *Second Marriage*. New York: W.W. Norton.

———. 1987. Couple's *Therapy Workbook*, Champaign, Illinois: Research Press.

Thomas, E.J. 1977. *Communication and Decision-Making: Analysis, Assessment and Change*. New York: Free Press.

Waring, E.M. 1981. Facilitating marital intimacy through self-disclosure. *The American Journal of Family Therapy* 9, 33–42.

Weick, K.E. 1984. Small wins. *American Psychologist* 39, 40–49.

Weingarten, H., and S. Leas. 1987. Levels of marital conflict model. *American Journal of Orthopsychiatry* 57, 407–17.

Weiss, R.L. 1978. The conceptualization of marriage and marriage disorders from a behavioral perspective. In T.J. Paolino and B.S. McCrady, eds. *Marriage and Marital Therapy: Psychoanalytic, Behavioral, and Systems Theory Perspectives*. New York: Brunner/Mazel.

Weiss, R.L., and G.R. Birchler. 1978. Adults with marital dysfunction. In M. Hersen and A. Bellack, eds. *Behavior Therapy in the Psychiatric Setting*. Baltimore: Williams and Williams.

Weiss, R.L., G.R. Birchler, and J.P. Vincent. 1974. Contractual models for negotiation training in marital dyads. *Journal of Marriage and the Family*, May, 321–30.

Weiss, R.L., H. Hops, and G.R. Patterson. 1973. A framework for conceptualizing marital conflict: A technology for altering it, some data for evaluating it. In L.A. Hamerlynck, L.D. Handy, and E.J. Mash, eds. *Behavior Change: Methodology, Concepts and Practice*. Champaign, Illinois: Research Press.

Weiss, R.L., and G. Margolin. 1970. Assessment of marital conflict and accord. In A.R. Ciminero, K.S. Calhoun, and H.E. Adams, eds. *Handbook of Behavioral Assessment*. New York: John Wiley and Sons.

Wile, D.B. 1981. *Couples Therapy: A Nontraditional Approach*. New York: John Wiley and Sons.

Wills, R.M., S.L. Faitler, and D.K. Snyder. 1987. Distinctiveness of behavioral versus insight-oriented marital therapy: An empirical analysis. *Journal of Consulting and Clinical Psychology* 55, 685–90.

Wills, T.A., R.L. Weiss, and G.R. Patterson. 1974. A behavioral analysis of the determinants of marital satisfaction. *Journal of Consulting and Clinical Psychology* 42, 802–11.

Zartman, I.W. 1978. *The Negotiation Process*. Beverly Hills, California: Sage Publications.

Zartman, I.W., and M.R. Berman. 1982. *The Practical Negotiator*. New Haven, Connecticut: Yale University Press.

Zimmer, D. 1983. Interaction patterns and communication skills in sexually distressed, maritally distressed and normal couples: Two experimental studies. *Journal of Sex and Marital Therapy* 4, 251–65.

DR. CONNIE PECK received her Ph.D. from the University of Wisconsin. Since then, she worked as a Psychologist at the University of Washington and later at La Trobe University in Australia, where for many years she was the Coordinator of the Psychology Clinic and taught in the graduate program in clinical psychology. She was the founding Chair of the La Trobe University Institute for Peace Research and the Founder and National Convener of Psychologists for the Prevention of War, a special interest group of the Australian Psychological Society. Dr. Peck has practiced, taught and written extensively in psychology, specializing in the area of conflict resolution and negotiation. She is the author of three other books and over fifty journal articles and book chapters. She is currently working at the United Nations Institute for Training and Research in Geneva, Switzerland where she organizes a course on dispute settlement for UN staff and diplomats.